P9-DVV-107

*Praise for*

# EVERYTHING IS HORRIBLE
# AND WONDERFUL

"Beautiful, funny, and epically poignant."

—Sarah Silverman

"Human and heartbreaking, this sister's story of living with and losing a brother to addiction is a doozy. A great read and an intimate and illuminating account of an addict's impact on a family."

—Bill Clegg, author of *Portrait of an Addict as a Young Man* and *Did You Ever Have a Family*

"Brutally honest and honestly beautiful, *Everything Is Horrible and Wonderful* is so much more than a story of how addiction can tear a family apart; it's a magnificent tribute to a brother and to the perfectly imperfect family that we all have. The clarity with which Stephanie Wittels Wachs describes addiction, death, and its aftermath comes through on every page. She lays bare the ugliest truths without demonizing the destructive behavior of an addict. Threaded through with the fiercest unconditional love, this is an absolutely gorgeous book."

—Matt Logelin, author of *Two Kisses for Maddy*

"Every minute, more of us know the unique pain of helplessly watching someone we care about descend into the pit of addiction. Stephanie Wittels Wachs has been there, and she emerges with her wit, wisdom, and spirit intact. This remarkable and movingly told story will break and mend hearts."

—David Sheff, author of *Beautiful Boy* and *Clean*

"Stephanie Wittels Wachs is honest, funny, moving, and so likable. She shows us the messy truth about losing someone you love—that there is no map for its tremendous pain and unexpected moments of joy."

—Kerry Cohen, author of *Loose Girl* and *Lush*

"A story about addiction and death cannot help but be sad (duh). But Steph has made this so much more than that. This is a book that hilariously and tenderly explores that unbreakable bond between siblings, a book that reminds you that your heart is mendable and malleable, even if it is broken."

—Nora McInerny, author of *It's Okay to Laugh:*
*(Crying Is Cool Too)*

# EVERYTHING IS HORRIBLE AND WONDERFUL

## A TRAGICOMIC MEMOIR OF GENIUS, HEROIN, LOVE, AND LOSS

### STEPHANIE WITTELS WACHS

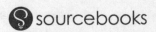

Published by Sourcebooks, Inc.
P.O. Box 4410, Naperville, Illinois 60567-4410
(630) 961-3900
Fax: (630) 961-2168
sourcebooks.com

Library of Congress Cataloging-in-Publication Data

Names: Wittels Wachs, Stephanie, author.
Title: Everything is horrible and wonderful : a tragicomic memoir of genius, heroin, love, and loss / Stephanie Wittels Wachs.
Description: Naperville, Illinois : Sourcebooks, [2018]
Identifiers: LCCN 2017046007 | (hardcover : alk. paper)
Subjects: LCSH: Wittels Wachs, Stephanie. | Wittels, Harris. | Drug addicts--Family relationships--United States. | Heroin abuse--United States. | Brothers and sisters--United States.
Classification: LCC HV5805 .W58 2018 | DDC 362.29/3092273--dc23 LC record available at https://lccn.loc.gov/2017046007

Printed and bound in the United States of America.
BVG 10 9 8 7 6 5 4 3 2 1

*For Harris and Iris*

# Foreword

by Aziz Ansari

When Stephanie first told me about the idea of her book, I thought it was fantastic. All the writing she had done since her brother's passing was so raw and honest, like her brother.

I had also found writing to be a helpful way to cope with Harris's sudden death. Days after his passing, I wrote a long piece trying to capture my favorite personal moments with Harris. It included anecdotes that many of his friends and colleagues shared the night of his passing. These were great stories that to me really encapsulated what was so unique and charming about Harris, and also what was so sad about losing him.

As I began to write this foreword, I soon realized I would never capture what I felt as I did when I first wrote down my thoughts of Harris passing days after.

It was cathartic for me and made me feel less helpless to attempt to share what I loved so much about my friend with a larger audience and try to give others a chance to learn of Harris through small, real moments.

When Stephanie and I spoke, we quickly decided my foreword would be best used to just showcase that piece as it was first posted.

We present it here unedited in its form from when I wrote it days after Harris passing. I hope this, and Stephanie's book, help give you a better picture of the very special person we lost.

Also, it makes me laugh to imagine Harris thinking, "So you just used the same thing you wrote a while ago as a foreword?! Laaaaaaazzzzyyyyy."

## RIP Harris Wittels. 1984–2015.

There are so few people that you meet in life that give you that feeling that you've found a real unique, original person. Harris Wittels was one of those and we lost him yesterday. He was 30 years old. I've been devastated.

I'm still waiting for the other phone call to let me know that Harris is okay and this was all a horrible misunderstanding. I don't know when my brain is going to be able to process the terrible feeling that fills my heart with dread and my eyes with tears every 20 seconds when I realize this very special person is really gone.

So, I wanted to write something to share my stories about Harris and what he meant to me.

I first knew Harris as a stand-up. I'd have him open shows quite a bit, and he was always fantastic. As his career as a writer took off, he got busy. He'd say that he didn't have time or wasn't working on stand-up at the time. Sadly, he had just started back working his stand-up, which made me thrilled as a fan. His stand-up, like his real-life personality, was open, honest (way more honest than how most people refer to *honest* in their stand-up), and hilarious.

As a writer, we worked on two films that never saw the light of day. The first was *Olympic Sized Asshole*. The premise was Danny McBride and I were two best friends who lived in South Carolina whose girl-friends had a three-way with a super-handsome star Olympic athlete (think Channing Tatum). We did a rough outline of it together, and then Harris went off to write the script.

Around this time in my career, I was very puzzled by film scripts. None of the ones I read ever made me laugh. I figured that I must not know how to read scripts properly. Maybe these things were funnier in person than on the page.

Then I got Harris's first draft of *Olympic*.

Every page had a huge laugh. I couldn't believe it. Jody Hill and I called each other and were just rolling about our favorite jokes.

I was *DYING*.

Here's a little chunk I found looking through old notes. The script was just full of great jokes like this:

```
                GLEN
Guys, I'm sorry. I can't give you
that promotion.


                FOREST
But we've been waiters here for
seven years.


                GLEN
There's a reason for that.


                KEVIN
Come on, Glen. You owe us. Who
lent you your first and last
month's rent for your new place?


                GLEN
You never did that.


                KEVIN
But I would. I'd do it in a sec-
ond. But I can't without a raise.
So just come on already.
```

Another bit I loved was when Danny's character and my character pitch a business idea in the beginning of the movie.

```
Forest clicks the first slide: A photo of Forest
seated on the toilet with his underwear still on.

                    KEVIN (CONT'D)
          What if I told you my friend
          Forest was taking a shit in
          that picture?


                    FOREST
          What am I thinking? Dropping two's
          with my underwear still on? I've
          lost my goddamned mind…or have I?


He clicks the next slide: a shot of him from behind
with a trap-door opening in his underwear.

                    KEVIN
          Let us introduce you to Shidderz.
          It's like the hole in your under-
          wear for peeing out of, but for
          dumps. Which is also the slogan.


A slide with a picture of the underwear and text
that reads: "Shidderz: It's like the hole for pee-
ing out of, but for dumps."

                    KEVIN (CONT'D)
          How many times has this happened to
          you? You're stumbling to the bath-
          room in the middle of the night.


                    (MORE)


                    KEVIN (CONT'D)
          You're disoriented, maybe still
          drunk. You have a time sensitive
          "shit"uation on your hands. You
          gotta get there quick, but also the
          bare ass on a toilet seat in the
          middle of the night can be a cold
          cold place. Normally, this would be
          a problem, but not for you - you're
          wearing Shidderz. Any questions?


HANES EMPLOYEE #1 raises his hand.
```

There was also a part that would be played by Paul Giamatti. I think this was something he just added as a last-minute addition that wasn't even in the outline.

```
        BRANDON, a chipper fellow in a Bozard's staff shirt
        who looks identical to Paul Giamatti enters.

                        FOREST (CONT'D)
                Paul Giamatti. No way!


        Toby gives Brandon a hug.

                        TOBY
                Hey, Brandon! Guys, this is my
                cousin, Brandon. He works here
                now.


                        BRANDON
                And lets lay all the questions to
                rest now. Yes, I got reconstruc-
                tive surgery to look like Paul
                Giamatti on that MTV show, "Make
                My Face Look Like That Guy's
                Face."


                        RAMON
                That's tight. I loved "Sideways,"
                fool.


                        BRANDON
                Believe me, I love it too. Sadly,
                this didn't really pan out finan-
                cially as I'd hoped. So here I am
                with you fine folks.


                        FOREST
                Not sure how you thought you were
                gonna make bank on that one, but
                you look like Paul Giamatti like
                a motherfucker. So good job.


        Kevin enters fuming.
```

Eventually, the project faded away as many movie projects tend to do.

But, after that, any time I worked on anything, I insisted that Harris Wittels be one of the writers. He was the first name I asked for every time. When I worked on the MTV Movie Awards. Those Randy videos for *Funny People*. Anytime I did a dumb commercial. Any time I needed to get joke writers, I always asked for Harris to help because he was truly the best of the best. And I was so lucky that he always said yes.

Most jokes when read by "comedy people" don't get a laugh per se. You just read it and go, "Oh that's funny" and you understand it would get a laugh. You eventually just know how jokes are constructed, and you aren't as easily surprised. Harris was part of that rare breed where you wouldn't see his shit coming. His jokes were so weird, unexpected, often brilliantly dumb that they were in that ultra-exclusive club of ones that made comedy people laugh—and laugh hard. This was why Harris was such a go-to for everyone. Anyone that was ever in a writers' room with him knew he was probably the funniest comedy writer out there. He was just a machine.

Remember the Obama-Galifianakis *Funny or Die* video?

> **GALIFIANAKIS**
> So, are you gonna run a third time?
>
> **OBAMA**
> I don't think that'd be a very good idea. That'd be like making a third *Hangover* movie.

I thought that was by far the best joke in that thing and maybe anything I watched last year. I found out today that it was a Wittels original. Of course.

Harris was also known as *the chuffah king*. *Chuffah* is the random nonsense characters in a scene talk about before getting to the meat of it that leads to story. Here's one of the best chuffah moments from *Parks* from the "Hunting Season" episode:

```
                TOM
      Your favorite kind of cake can't
      be birthday cake; that's like say-
      ing your favorite kind of cereal
      is breakfast cereal.


               DONNA
      I love breakfast cereal.
```

Harris excelled at coming up with hilarious, random nonsense like this. It was a tool that no one else seemed to have. I'm not a big podcast listener, but today I found out this was also kind of the fuel for Harris's Foam Corner (or Harris's Phone Corner) from *Comedy Bang! Bang!* podcast. Here's a playlist that is filled with this kind of hilarious, awful nonsense from Harris: https://www.youtube.com/playlist?list=PLBB4729D88A16451A.

Here's some highlights I found on Tumblr today:

"One time I said to a guy that 'I loved learning new things. I'm a bit of an infomaniac.' And he thought I said NYMPHOMANIAC... so he fucked me. And I said 'No, no, no... I said INFO. I'm an INFOmaniac' And he said 'Well, here's some info...you just got fucked. Clean yourself up.'"

"I hate smoking sections. Unless it's Jim Carrey's *The Mask*. Then the smoking section is my favorite part!"

"I'm not getting married until gay people can get married. Because I'm gay."

Imagine being around a guy who was this uniquely silly all the damn time. That's what it was like being in a writers' room with Harris. It was just bullshit like this nonstop. And it was the best.

After we failed to get *Olympic* off the ground, we had another idea called *Big Time*. This was about myself and another guy becoming super-famous after a video of us saving a bunch of little black kids from a burning fire went viral. Again, the plan was that Harris and I would draft a story (this time with our friend Jason Woliner) and then Harris would bang out the script.

One of my favorite Harris stories was before writing this script we'd pitch the story to studios. In one part of the pitch, we had a bit where the two leads became quasi-famous and started attending B-level celeb parties. In describing this scene in our practice session, Harris would say, "Guys like Chris Pontius would be there." I'd say, "Alright Harris, none of these execs know who Chris Pontius from *Jackass* is, don't say that."

At that point, he knew he had me. Every pitch—and keep in mind these are important pitches with studio heads, etc.—I would lead and then as soon as I got to that scene, he would throw it in with glee, "You know, guys like Pontius would be there." He even dropped the *Chris* and was just saying *Pontius*. Last name only. Jason and I were dying.

Then, in an even more absurd move, he added a second part to this bit. During the pitch, he started saying, "Then the guys get famous, and they do all the talk shows: *Letterman…Conan…Pontius Tonight…*" To be clear, *Pontius Tonight* is a fictional show hosted by Chris Pontius that he made up just to make me laugh/fume. He said that execs would assume this was a real thing as to not seem out of touch. It was great. Harris would rather make all of us laugh than worry about jeopardizing these meetings.

He really seemed to relish getting laughs out of other comedians. Last night, the *Parks* writers staff and other friends shared

Harris stories. One of my favorites was there was a serious email from NBC about a big sexual harassment seminar. Serious execs are cc'd along with Harris and the writers. Harris writes back, REPLY ALL, with this gem—now keep in mind EVERYONE is on this email, all the crew, so many higher-level producers and execs. Here we go:

---

**NBC Mandatory Workplace Harassment Meeting**

A brief reminder that we all have to attend a mandatory NBC Workplace Harassment Seminar this Friday, July 22nd at 8am here at the lot.

It will be downstairs in the basement Multi Purpose Room #1

there will be bagels.

and coffee

Thanks!

---

**harris wittels**

Will the bagels be shaped like pussy holes?

Sent from an old rotary telephone

---

As both our movies fizzled, Harris and I worked together on *Parks and Rec*. I was so thrilled when he got hired to be a writer, and the episodes where he was on set were ones I looked forward to. A writer on set would pitch alternate jokes and help you if you felt a scene didn't work, who better than Harris in that situation? Talking to other writers on the show today, it was clear Harris's contribution to the world of

Pawnee was immense. I'm sure he wrote many of the lines that made you laugh throughout the show. Harris also eventually acted in the show as one of the animal control guys.

I also want to say, besides being so unbelievably hilarious, Harris was truly a sweet guy. He was so lovable even when saying the most disgusting things. You just couldn't help but love him. He had the most ridiculous opinions on everything from food to dating to music, and he'd defend them to no end. He loved to make ridiculous boasts that he insisted he could achieve. Here are a few that I compiled:

* Do as good a job as Trent Reznor scoring *The Social Network*
* Play against the Lakers and juke NBA point guard Steve Blake
* Hit an NBA 3-pointer
* Play right field in a Major League Baseball game, and catch a pop-up, and easily throw it back to the infield
* Act as well as any actor
* Every girl has, at minimum, a 20% crush on him

He was once adamant that he could taste the difference between all the major water bottle brands—and he did! He also once claimed he could beat anyone in the entire *Parks* offices at arm wrestling. Mike Schur gleefully egged him on: "Really, Harris? Anyone?" Harris said, "Yeah." Then Mike beckoned John Valerio—a giant, muscular man with enormous arms—who worked in the editing department. Harris: "Shit! I forgot about Valerio. Come on, man!" Nevertheless, Harris went through with the match, put up a good fight, and was extremely gracious in defeat.

He was also kind of an odd ladies' man in a way. Not blessed with a tall stature and traditional handsome-guy stuff, he was able to transcend it all by being charming in an adorable/silly way. He was a romantic at heart. He once had a really big date. Someone way out of his league. His move: show up with a box of Russell Stover chocolates. You know, the brand of chocolates you get when you really want to impress a girl. He also once sent an e-vite to a girl's heart. She declined. He once proposed to a woman on G-Chat. Genuinely.

Here's some other random things I loved about him: He loved 311 and knew that the bassist's name was P-Nut. He once had dinner with my parents and me in New York at a fancy restaurant and showed up in a suit that was 5 sizes too big. He looked like a kid dressing up in his dad's clothes. Afterward, he turned to me and said, "Hey man, can you help me get a suit that fits?" His Tinder profile said, "I make money. I'll buy you a couch." We asked him why and he said, "Girls love couches." He would always order the most unabashedly unhealthy, grossest thing at lunch. The most legendary being a burger he once ordered at *Parks* that had fried egg, bacon, avocado, onion rings (these are *ON* the burger FYI), BBQ sauce, and Monterey Jack cheese. He would take 4 things of mozzarella string cheese, line 'em up, and melt it in the microwave. And then he'd eat this with a fork for a snack. I would always try to order healthy. Once I suggested a vegetarian place. After the email went out, I got a text from him: "Guys this vegan place is an atrocity. Please reconsider." He once left the writers' office for lunch to eat at his house and texted my brother Aniz that he was "making Chili's leftovers at home." It really made me laugh that he chose the word *making* to describe heating up disgusting leftovers. He loved Chili's but could never get anyone to join him. He would often go on solo missions. He once went to Chili's by himself in Encino, and Joe Mande asked him why Encino and not the closer one, in Inglewood. He said, "The good one's in Encino, you gotta go out to Encino."

Weirdly, besides *Parks*, a lot of the stuff we worked on together never made it out into the world.

Another harsh part of this tragedy is that was all about to change. Around the time *Parks* was ending, I started developing a new project with my friend Alan Yang, another writer on *Parks*. Immediately, we knew we wanted Harris to help us write it. We were lucky to get him on board, and for the past 5 months or so, he's been an integral part of this new project. He worked tirelessly and was a leader on our staff, and we were all thrilled to be doing this thing that was actually going forward.

We knew Harris had issues with addiction, but things were pointing in the right direction. He was getting treatment and focused on his career and the opportunities ahead. It all seemed to point in the right direction. We were all about to move to New York together in March to have great fun and make great work. He was excited. I was excited. It all seemed perfect. He just found an apartment on Monday.

Then, I got the most horrific phone call yesterday. I couldn't comprehend it.

This week I spent a lot of time with Harris. On Monday he drove me to a dinner we were having. His iPod was on shuffle and every fucking song was a different Phish bootleg. I kept forcing him to skip until it was Phish maybe covering another more tolerable band's song. Then we hit a band called Pralines and Dick. I told him this was particularly bad. He let me know it was his high school jam band and warned me about the upcoming 5-minute funk breakdown. I couldn't help but enjoy it.

I was so excited for what was ahead for Harris. I knew he was going to really explode after this new project. The little bit of Wittels comedy out there was just the tip of the tip of the iceberg. He had so much more to give, and I was so excited for him. He seemed to be turning things around. He asked me for help finding a nutritionist.

He said he knew nothing about nutrition. I informed him that I could confirm Chili's is pretty bad for you. He even reluctantly ordered the "vegan bowl" for lunch the day before he passed when we were all writing together.

My last memory of him was from that day.

We were punching up a script. In punch up, you're just trying to beat jokes that maybe aren't landing. Everyone contributes and tries to beat the joke, and you leave the best one in. But for us, what would happen is, basically, all the writers would pitch something, then Harris would chime in with something so bizarre and hilarious it would either make it in or make us laugh, and we'd agree it was the most hilarious but probably too crazy. That last day, I remember I hit a line and we needed a better joke. I was exhausted. I turned to Harris and just wanted him to fix it so we could move on. I yelled, "Harris! I need you, get off your phone. Make this joke better, fix it please." And, of course, he did.

Bye, Harris. I miss you, and I'm glad I got to enjoy your genuinely amazing and original presence. I wish I got to you know even more. I hope people reading this realize what an incredibly unique man you were, and what brutal a loss it is for those who knew you and also for those who never had the pleasure. This has been so hard to write because I just keep wanting to add more and more stories and more jokes and more everything, but I'd never be able to finish it. You are far too special to sum up in any kind of piece like this. You were one of the best, and we all will miss you.

*Love,*
*Aziz*

# 01
—

## Day One

*He's dead.*
*He died.*
*Your brother died.*
*He is dead.*

I can't recall the exact phrase. She definitely used some tense of *to die* and not some other euphemism for *permanently gone from your life from this point forward*. She didn't say, "Your brother passed away." Passing away is too natural, too *as it should be*. Passing away is what my grandmother did in her sleep at ninety-two after living a complete life. It was sad. And expected.

This isn't that.

This is brutal and tragic and worthy of Irish keening.

You can't be dead.

You emailed Mom earlier that night. You described the place you would sublet in New York. You said the *Parks and Recreation* series finale would make her cry. You said you felt "very fortunate." You told her you loved her.

You are coming home next weekend to see your niece. She just started walking. You were so excited.

You are supposed to be coming home.

You are supposed to be coming home *alive*.

It's five minutes after five o'clock on February 19, 2015. I'm changing the baby's diaper in the bathroom of the Center for Hearing and Speech when the phone rings. It's an unknown LA area code. I press ignore and continue to deal with the dirty diaper.

I'm in a notably good mood. Iris just killed it at her monthly speech therapy session. Mike and I radiate pride and joy. Also, my thirty-fourth birthday is tomorrow, and we've actually made plans. Mom and Dad will come over with Star Pizza and birthday cake. Knowing Mom, it'll be a white sheet cake with white icing from the grocery store. I'll blow out my candles and make a wish, then Mike and I will put Iris to bed and head to a neighborhood tiki bar with adult friends to drink colorful drinks out of ceramic mugs that are lit on fire. A truly rare occasion. I'm ready.

The phone rings again. Same unknown LA number.

*I have imagined this moment before.*

I answer.

"Is this Stephanie Wittels?"

"Yes."

"Is Harris Wittels your brother?"

"Yes."

2

"When was the last time you spoke to your brother?"

"I don't know. Why? What's going on? I'm changing my baby's diaper."

"Is there another adult with you?"

*"Why? What happened? No! Wait. WAIT!"*

I scream for Mike down the hall. He runs in and grabs the waist-down naked baby, who is now shrieking.

And then she tells me:


*He's dead.*
*He died.*
*Your brother died.*
*He is dead.*


I fall onto the faded blue tile of the bathroom floor, screaming and crying in agony. The detective remains on the phone, reciting her lines about being sorry and needing to ask me a few questions. The baby won't stop shrieking, so I push myself off the bathroom floor and rush down the long hallway toward the entrance to the building. The few people left at work stare, confused. It's a lot of emotion for five o'clock on a Thursday. When I head outside, it's jarring to see that the world is still turning. Everyone is still doing all of the things they normally do at rush hour: driving, talking, texting, honking. The sun is shining. It's a beautiful day. Tragedy always strikes on a beautiful day.

I fall to my hands and knees again and pound my fists on the pavement. (I literally do this.) Mike rushes outside and embraces me on the ground like a blanket. "Oh God!" he cries.

I manage to continue holding the phone to my ear while the detective provides details:

"…A balloon. A spoon. A syringe cap but no needle…" She asks questions: "Was he suicidal?"

"No."

"Did he have any medical issues?"

"Yes. He was a drug addict."

*A balloon, a spoon, a syringe. Obviously, he was a fucking drug addict.*

"I tried to contact your mother but couldn't reach her," she says.

I realize at this point that I'll have to tell Mom her only son is dead and *that* would be the most horrific moment of my life—even more horrific than this one.

The detective tells me to call her with any questions, and I hang up the phone.

Still sobbing, I dig the car keys out of my purse and notice the baby isn't in Mike's arms. "She's with Amy," he says. Her speech therapist. "She's okay."

I keep repeating that I have to get to my parents. Mike tries to reason with me that I am in no condition to drive, but I am currently unreasonable and get in the car anyway. Somehow, I navigate the familiar way to our parents' building while carrying the most unfamiliar sickness in my gut.

Dad is walking up from the parking garage as I pull into the driveway of their high-rise. Once I say the thing I have come to say, his world will collapse like mine just did. We sit on a smooth concrete bench outside the building. He's right beside me, but there's a chasm between us. He's on one side, and I'm on the other. Tell me, how does one say a thing like this? How does a person tell another person his youngest child is dead? How would you write this scene—the scene where I destroy our father with a single sentence? I say it in between sobs. I don't remember how. His face goes blank. A tear falls out of his eye, but he says nothing.

Mom isn't home. She's out with friends: a movie and an early dinner. Dad and I take the elevator to their unit on the seventeenth floor and sit on the couch, shifting between intermittent sobs and silence. I grip the phone, unsure of what to do with it, then pace the floor, hysterical, while Mom enjoys her final moments of ignorant bliss. Mike comes in with Iris, who always gets hysterical when I get hysterical, so I try to stay calm.

Your business manager calls, and I scurry down the hall to Mom's bedroom. I sit at her desk, so neatly organized, and scratch down some notes on her Houston SPCA notepad.

He is notably kind. He sends condolences. He says he was at your LA home today when the detectives arrived. He says something about a coroner's notice being affixed to the front door of the house, telling the world you have died. He tells me he doesn't want to rush me and knows this is a deeply personal time for our family, but that once the news gets out, it will be a runaway train out of our control. He says I need to tell my mom as soon as possible.

I don't fully understand what he means. You are my brother. You are my brother who died. I don't realize who you are to everyone else.

Mom is still not fucking home. I don't know what to do.

I text her and ask where she is. She says she's at some sushi restaurant and texts me a picture of her dinner.

I ask if she's playing cards later tonight.

She asks why—what's wrong?

I say nothing.

It's 6:45 when the phone rings, less than two hours since I spoke to the detective. It's one of your best friends, Matt Marcus, who rarely/never calls me. He asks if it's true. He tells me TMZ leaked the story.

TMZ leaked the fucking story before my mother can find out her only son is dead.

Finally, she is downstairs in the parking garage. She has gotten several texts. *Several people have texted her about her son who has died.* She calls me, panicked. She asks what's going on. Her voice teeters on the edge of hysterics, high-pitched and shaky. I tell her to stay put. I'll be right down. I sprint down the long hallway to the elevator, but she's already on her way up as I am on my way down, and we miss each other. I get back on the elevator. I sprint back to their apartment.

Dad has already broken the news. I don't know how.

She wails and wails and wails.

*"Why? No! Not my baby! Oh God, NOT MY BABY!"*

Her knees buckle.

She melts to the floor.

She pounds the floor.

She curls into the fetal position. She literally does this.

I hold her.

We cry.


People show up within the hour. They say various things at me. I retain none of it. The phone rings and dings a thousand times.

I just sit on the couch, stare at the wall, and cry.

The night goes on for a lifetime. At some point, Mike drives us home. I take one of my Ambien, prescribed as needed, and cry myself to sleep.

## 02
—

## Before

March 2013

I learned Harris was a drug addict at five o'clock on a sunny Thursday afternoon in March, two years and eighteen days before he died. I was chopping cherry tomatoes in the galley kitchen of our tiny apartment on the bottom floor of a red-brick Houston fourplex. Martha Stewart has this recipe for one-pot pasta—it's sublime. My wedding was three days away.

Soon, Mike and I would walk down the aisle to the *Friday Night Lights* theme song and spill our teary wedding vows under a beautiful, handmade lace chuppah. We would eat truffled macaroni and cheese and get day-drunk on the open bar and dance the Hava Nagila to the accompanying mariachi band. We would look around the room every fifteen minutes and be awestruck by all the love in this one place, at this one time. After the wedding, Mike and I would eat leftover wedding cake with plastic forks out of to-go containers in our hotel suite.

But first, I answered the phone.

It was Harris. We texted constantly, but he rarely called unless there was girl drama. I worried for a moment that he was calling to tell me he and his girlfriend (who was coming to the wedding) had broken up. This would have been par for the course, as he'd been in a series of toxic relationships since college that always seemed to end badly. But this relationship was different. It was the first healthy, long-term relationship he'd ever been in. They'd met at a party nine months before and, from that point forward, were inseparable. Although it couldn't be possible, she seemed devoid of flaws. In his eyes—and in ours—she was perfect. A funny, creative, kind, beautiful musician who made him mix tapes and put up with—even indulged in—his shitty, fast-food eating habits. What a loss. And terrible timing.

Instead, he told me he was a drug addict.

And that he'd been spending roughly $4,000 a month on pills. Oxycontin, specifically. And that he planned to "work on it."

Three days before my wedding.

None of this made any sense. We came from a good family. My dad, Ellison, was a doctor; my mom, Maureen, the PTO president. She chaperoned every field trip and minivanned us to and from all of our many after-school activities. We went to summer camps and Disney World. We all genuinely liked each other. Growing up, Harris was my loyal sidekick even though I constantly forced him to dress up in women's clothing, wear makeup, and play various roles in the plays I'd create to be performed in our living room. Our house was always full of laughter. Much to my mother's dismay, my dad, Harris, and I used to have epic water fights in the kitchen using the spray hose on the sink. Once, my mother sent us both to charm school. At one point during the culminating recital, Harris and I confidently picked up the water bowls meant for hand-washing and drank out of them like animals. Harris loved that story.

My brother, three years and three months my junior, was the success story every Jewish mother ached to brag about at her weekly mah-jongg game: a Hollywood wonder-kid who landed his first professional TV writing job on The Sarah Silverman Program at twenty-two years old—only six months out of college after she saw him doing stand-up in LA. Although unusual—the stuff that myths are made of, really—it wasn't all that shocking. If anyone could fit into this dream scenario, it was Harris.

His career trajectory seemed preordained. He told his first joke at three years old. It was the summer of 1988. We were snacking in the kitchen of my mom's best friend's house. She mentioned Harris County, where we grew up in Houston, Texas. Reflexively, as if he was put on this earth for this moment and thousands more like it, he shouted, "I not Harris County, I Harris Wittels!" The whole room died laughing. He killed at the age of three.

And his whole life, he just kept chasing that high. As a seven-year-old, he would draw smiley faces on his butt, stick a toothbrush in it, and do entire monologues—out of his butt—for the family. He was part of a sketch comedy troupe in high school called Will Act for Food, WAFF for short. They rented out a small theater for their first live-sketch show, and midway through, Harris meandered across the stage totally naked, wearing nothing but a cowboy hat over his loins. Our grandmother was in the audience. I remember, years later, she wore the same befuddled face watching his first Showtime comedy special, where he did this bit about jerking off when you have a roommate, and how you have to keep checking to make sure the roommate isn't awake, so it really amounts to jerking off to your roommate.

His grades weren't great in school, but not for a lack of intrinsic motivation. A staunch academic, our dad was always pushing him to do better, but Harris refused to do things that didn't make him happy. Rather, he played drums in his high school band, Pralines and Dik, and spent countless hours consuming every comedy special or sitcom he could find on TV or at Blockbuster, his spiritual home. He idolized Louis C.K. and Mitch Hedberg. Hedberg would go on to die of a drug overdose at thirty-seven years old, and Louis C.K. would be accused of sexual misconduct by a number of women. Regardless, these were the giants who, despite their demons, influenced Harris to become who he was.

When we were teenagers, our parents took us to see them on two separate occasions at the Laff Stop, this infamous, little comedy club in Houston that no longer exists. After Louis's set, Harris approached him at the bar and, in all seriousness, told Louis he could give him some notes on how to be funnier. He was always fearless. Mostly fearless. I remember he used to throw up before going on stage. He threw up constantly as a child. When we were kids, stomach cramps were his go-to excuse to leave anywhere he no longer wanted to be. In high school, he'd chug Kaopectate for breakfast nearly every morning. One time in college, I saw him hang up the phone after a moderately tense conversation with a girlfriend and immediately vomit.

Despite the naturally nervous stomach, Harris started doing open mics as soon as he turned eighteen and could legally enter the clubs without our parents. The whole summer before leaving for college, he got up every Monday night at the Laff Stop, where he'd seen his idols years before. I remember sitting in the audience for these mostly terrible shows, nervously waiting for his name to be called. During his set, I would laugh uncomfortably hard at all his jokes and look around to make sure everyone else was doing the same. He used to tell this one joke about potato shoes that I can still hear in my head in his exact intonation: "Do you think a homeless guy ever went up to another homeless guy and accidentally asked *him* for some change? Excuse me, can you spare some change? Um, can *you* spare some change?! Oh, hey Terry didn't see ya there! You like my new shoes? They're old. You like my new shoes? They're potatoes!"

When he got to Emerson College in Boston, he majored in television and video but continued to focus on comedy. He did regular open mics at the Comedy Studio in Harvard Square and started a bizarro sketch comedy group called Fancy Pants with college friends Noah Garfinkel, Jim Hanft, Joe Mande, Gabe Rothschild, and Armen Weitzman.

During Harris's last semester at Emerson, he opted for an internship at Comedy Central in LA. It didn't take long for all the executives to start stopping by the intern's desk to get advice on what was and wasn't funny. Harris was a living comedy encyclopedia, the Little Man Tate of the comedy world. After the internship ended, he remained in LA and got a day job being a nanny to two little French boys. But at night, it was all comedy. He signed up for classes at Upright Citizens Brigade and continued going to every open mic he could find.

In May 2006, fresh out of college, he got a spot on UCB's *Comedy Death-Ray* hosted by Scott Aukerman of *Comedy Bang! Bang!* Scott would go on to become one of Harris's dearest friends and closest collaborators, but at the time, he'd never met Harris nor seen his act and was skeptical because Harris was essentially a newborn baby. However, a mutual friend convinced Scott to put him on the show with Doug Benson, Sarah Silverman, Paul F. Tompkins, Tig Notaro, and Blaine Capatch. According to Scott, Harris killed. At twenty-two, on a line-up like that, he made his mark.

Harris was that rare person whose childhood dreams turned into adult realities. He always knew what he wanted to do and *actually did it*. Being whip-smart, funny, hardworking, and endlessly charming contributed to his success, but it's also worth noting that he'd always been lucky. He was the asshole who left his cell phone in a New York City cab only to have the cabbie drive it back to my Queens apartment hours later just to return it to him. When he was in college, he lost his wallet in the Boston bus terminal and someone mailed it to our permanent address in Texas with all the cash *still in it*.

Six months after doing the *Comedy Death-Ray* show, Harris got an email from Sarah Silverman asking if he'd be interested in writing for her new Comedy Central show:

> Okay, so we have a slot open to write on the next season of my show. Do you have anything we can read? My producer will contact you about it, but I wanted to give you a heads up. Flanny loves you and I thought you were GREAT when I saw you. Don't know what you are looking to do, but if this potentially interests you, submit something—anything—if you think it represents how you write or come up with ideas.
>
> If this isn't what you are looking to do PLEASE don't think twice. It was just a thought. Always good to have a young smart silly greenie in the room is all. But if you're not looking to write on a show, it's not like it would be awkward next time we bump into each other or something.
>
> s

According to Harris, she escorted him to a big, fancy business lunch a few weeks later to meet the studio executives. Knowing that he was twenty-two and totally out of his element, she literally grabbed him by the arm and mentored him through each new handshake. "Harris, this is so and so, shake his hand. Harris, this is so and so, shake his hand." And it worked. He booked the job as the "young smart silly greenie in the room."

From there, Harris's career trajectory was swift and steep. After two seasons on *The Sarah Silverman Show*, he got hired as a staff writer on Season 2 of *Parks and Recreation*, where he remained for the next six years, eventually working his way up to the title of co-executive producer. In his spare time, he wrote for *Eastbound & Down* and became a notorious podcaster with popular shows like *Analyze Phish*, *Comedy Bang! Bang!*, and *Farts and Procreation*. He did stand-up on the *Jimmy Kimmel Show* and opened for Sarah, Aziz Ansari, and Louis C.K.

At the time Harris died, he was a thirty-year-old co-executive producer on a beloved, major network television show. He had invented the word *humblebrag*, which earned him a book deal and a spot in the English dictionary. He had written jokes for President Obama that the president delivered in Zach Galifianakis's *Between Two Ferns*, which has been viewed on YouTube more than twenty million times.

How many people can say that?

On the phone with Harris that March day, I tried to stay calm and judgment-free.

"Do you plan to go to rehab?" I asked.

He said he couldn't. *Parks* was shooting through June. He had to be in LA for work. He planned to tackle this on his own. He could do it. It was under control.

Also: "Don't tell Mom and Dad—please don't tell Mom and Dad," he insisted. He didn't want to worry them. He only wanted to worry *me*. Three days before my wedding. Best to just keep this secret safe like we'd always done. He'd see me at the wedding, he said. He was excited! Yay! Don't worry. "I'll be fine. Love you, sister."

I hung up and cried into Mike's shirt while standing beside the kitchen table. I always knew my brother was a recreational drug user but had no idea it had gotten to the point where he *needed* them. I knew he'd been having severe back pain and was taking painkillers. The pain was so bad, he had been rushed to the emergency room one night in an ambulance. He and I had seen this storyline on one of our favorite TV shows, *Intervention*, countless times. Back pain + painkillers = drug addiction. And yet here we were.

It was a lot to take in three days before my wedding. It was a lot to take in, period.

Harris gave it his all that weekend, but there was a cloudy film over the lens. He smiled with his mouth and not his eyes, like in one of those tests of all the smiling faces where you pick the genuinely happy people and the sad people. He was always a little distant, a little withdrawn, and smoking or pacing excessively, but the distance felt wider and it was more of a palpable bummer on the happiest day of my life. I didn't get the impression, however, that anyone else noticed. Harris had years of professional experience being outwardly charming and carefree when he felt like a tense little ball of toxic waste on the inside. That's essentially what it is to *be* a comedian. Plus, my parents were just thrilled blind that he was there with his girlfriend. My mom insisted that she be in all the family photos that day.

Second to Mike's wedding vows—which began with the sentence "You are strange"...*swoon*—Harris's toast was my favorite speech of the day. It was a classic sort of toast that only a little brother could give to his big sister:

*Hello everybody. I'm Harris—I'm the brother. So, my sister— she basically raised me. And by raised, I mean tortured me. She would dress me up in girl clothes and make me do her weird plays she wrote, and she'd play with my Hanukkah presents first. One time, her and Jennifer tried to trick me into drinking my own pee. They pretended that it was their pee, but it was apple juice, and then they made me go in a cup, too. But I knew. I didn't do it…til later.*

*And then we grew up, and she befriended me. And by befriended I mean she taught me how to be delinquent. She taught me how to sneak out of the house without the alarm going off. She'd throw me a few extra beers if her and her friends didn't want them. She taught me how to hide contraband in the back of my stereo, where the batteries go. It's a big slot back there, and you can fit a lot of stuff. And I worshipped her and thought she was the coolest. She shopped at the Value Village resale shop, and so I shopped there, too, 'cause I wanted her to think I was cool, which is disgusting. It's a horrible cesspool of germs and armpit stains and I went through just so she'd like me.*

*And then we became adults, and I think that's when we actually became real friends and equals. And, you know, she's the person I could always talk to the most, and I always counted on her for anything. And even when I was busy becoming a Hollywood douchebag, she would always check in on me and force me to stay in touch, and I'm glad that we did.*

*You know, she's obviously very thoughtful and caring, and she deserves someone that's equally thoughtful and caring, and I think she found that in Mike. They are a perfect fit. Stephanie goes one hundred miles per hour and Mike, he goes a cool thirty miles per hour, so between them, they're going sixty-five, and that's a good speed. So, I'm glad that I got a brother and our family got bigger, and I love you guys. Congrats.*

I cackled my way to tears, and before he took his seat, I hugged him with all of the love I had in my body, which was the only thing that existed inside of me on that glorious day.

I was so happy.

## 03

—

## Week One

I didn't know it was possible to awaken from a state of sleep in tears, but the morning after your death, I learn that it is. It's my thirty-fourth birthday, but Facebook doesn't understand that I'm not in the mood to celebrate anything ever again. Every time I log on, a window pops up with an exploding firework graphic and a happy birthday banner that displays all the wall posts about your death. I tell Mike to take my birthday off the calendar for the duration of our lives.

Over the next few days, we all want to die but make arrangements instead.

We meet with the funeral director. Talk programs. Select pall-bearers. Pick out burial clothes: a Phish T-shirt, your favorite reindeer pajama bottoms, house slippers, and a Phish hat. We choose a casket out of a binder with plastic sheet covers that the funeral director presents. It's traditional to bury a Jewish person in a plain, pine box, but Mom insists on something nicer.

We meet with the current rabbi of our synagogue who married Mike and me two years before and the retired rabbi, who Bar/Bat Mitzvahed both of us as children. Do you remember after your speech when he told the audience to look for this kid at the Laff Stop some day? You were always you. The rabbis will co-lead the service. During the recessional, we'll play "Once in a While," our favorite Don't Stop or We'll Die song. That was your band, and you loved playing drums in it more than almost anything, so it feels appropriate.

In a way, this is all just like directing a play. A *very* depressing play.

Everyone decides that I should deliver your eulogy. Mom and Dad always said I spoke for you the first five years of your life—they thought maybe you were mute—so I guess it's fitting that I speak for you now. *Somehow*. I spend hours working on it. Remembering, writing, revising; remembering, writing, revising; remembering, writing, revising. When Mike prints out the final draft for me, the cover page logs twenty-six hours of work. Meanwhile, Mike writes an obituary that is beautiful and poignant, but the newspaper sends an invoice for $2,563.72, which is fucking lunacy. It's like that scene from *The Big Lebowski* where the snooty funeral director tries to sell John Goodman's character an urn for $180, and he shouts, "Just because we're bereaved doesn't make us *saps*!" Then he pounds his fist on the desk and transports the ashes in a Folgers coffee can. Mike edits the obituary down to $1,406.34.

People keep asking where they can make a donation. These are the sorts of things you have to figure out when a person you love dies. We all agree on a scholarship fund at the High School for the Performing and Visual Arts, where I currently teach acting full-time. You and I both graduated from the theatre department, and you always loved to come talk to my students when you were in town. It feels like a good fit. I call my boss, the principal of the school, to hash out the details. In the same conversation, I tell him I'm not sure when I'll be coming back to work. He tells me to take all the time I need. I wonder if forever is an option.

You also made me the executor of your estate, a demanding job for which I never applied. Over the course of the week, I sign various documents. Turns out, you had created a living trust several years ago that was completely squared away and in order when you died. Not a single string was left untied. Fifty percent of your estate will go to me, and fifty percent will go to Mom and Dad. Your business manager said it's extremely unusual for his clients, especially the young, creative ones, to be this detailed with post-death arrangements. Mike and I have an actual child and don't even have a will yet. I make a mental note to call the attorney and schedule an appointment to get that done once the dust settles. *If* the dust ever settles.

All the while, we try to coordinate with the funeral home in Houston, the detective, and the coroner's office in LA. The coroner won't release your body until they complete an autopsy, and there are too many dead people in line.

So, we wait.

Meanwhile, people come and go. They bring deli. It feels wrong.

When an old person dies, it makes sense for people to visit, nosh on corned beef, and make small talk. But not now. Not when a young, talented, brilliant, remarkable person has died. True tragedy transcends small talk. The occasion, however, hasn't stopped Dad from being Dad, and he's still trying his best to do the "polite host" routine. He keeps perfunctorily asking people how they are, and they keep carelessly responding with the latest news about their children and grandchildren. To a man who's just lost his own child and future grandchildren. If you were here, you'd comment on what a fucked-up scene this is.

My fuse is particularly short. I don't want to hug or commiserate or cry on another shoulder. I have no tolerance for social conventions.

Anyone who asks, "How are you?" is met with "Terrible—my brother just died." Some version of this sentence keeps running through my mind like a newsfeed on the bottom of a screen. It never stops. It underscores every moment: "My brother is dead, my brother is dead, my brother is dead, my brother is dead, my brother is dead, my brother is dead, my brother is dead, my brother is dead, my brother is dead…"

Like I have to keep saying it or it isn't real. Like I have to keep reminding myself that this is really happening because it's just too fucking unbelievable.

More unbelievable is that your death is a now a trending topic on social media. My entire Facebook feed is you—photos, articles, podcasts, videos, quotes, blog posts, tweets. On Instagram, the hashtag *#harriswittels* brings up hand-drawn sketches and paintings by strangers, tribute photos of you doing stand-up and playing the recurring role of Harris, the animal control guy, on *Parks and Rec* captioned with favorite quotes like "I hate smoking sections—unless we're talking about the movie *The Mask* with Jim Carrey, then the smoking section is my favorite part." Someone has sketched a detailed black-and-white picture of you and made it into a sticker with a caption that reads *Humble Living: Harris Wittels (1984–2015)*. People are pasting them all over LA, taking photos of them whenever spotted, and posting the photos online. It's like a game: Find the Harris Wittels memorial sticker.

To see it unfold in this way is simultaneously comforting and horrifying. Your death is not just something we are able to deal with privately as a family; it's something people are grieving publicly and "liking" on Facebook. The Westboro Baptist Church is literally standing outside the offices of *LA Weekly* holding protest signs that say *God Hates Fag Enablers*, *Repent or Perish*, and *Harris In Hell*. It's sick as fuck, although a spectacle you would have likely enjoyed. Your friend Joe Mande sums it up best on Twitter: "Goddammit, Harris, the Westboro Baptist Church just called you a 'fag enabler' and you're not here to see it."

I keep thinking about what your business manager said when I spoke to him in those first few hours, that once the news got out it would be a runaway train, out of our control. It didn't register at the time. I knew you were successful, but you were always so casual and humble about your career that I didn't realize just quite how much you meant to everyone else. Yet another layer to wrap my broken head around.

By Day Five, the waiting for your body to come home becomes so insufferable that I storm out of the living room screaming and crying at the top of my lungs as if I'm a thirteen-year-old girl in the midst of a temper tantrum: "I'm sick of waiting! This is *bullshit*! We need to bury him. We need to bury him *now*! *I don't want to fucking wait anymore!* I DON'T WANT TO DO THIS ANYMORE!" No one pays me any attention. This sort of climactic outburst belongs in the scene.

Not that we are super religious, but in Judaism, it's customary to bury a loved one within forty-eight hours. And in Judaism, the customs are really the point. It takes seven days to complete the autopsy and fly you back home to Houston, where you will be buried beside the plots Mom and Dad bought for themselves, thinking they'd be in the ground long before either of us.

The day before the funeral, I realize I have nothing to wear. I have to go to a store where people are buying dresses for happy occasions and buy a dress *to wear to your funeral*, a dress that will forever hang in my closet as the dress I wore to my brother's funeral. I'll never wear it again, but I won't ever give it away. It will just hang there, sadly and forever, as a daily reminder that things can always be worse.

# 04

—

## Week Two

The sun sets and rises as it somehow continues to do, and it's time to bury you in the ground.

The scene is equal parts sad and surreal.

The shiny black limousines.

The collision of silence and noise inside of my head and the inability to take a deep breath.

The paralysis at the door of the chapel after being hit by the sudden impact of the crowd. Once I go in, I must sit through your funeral, and I don't want to sit through your funeral. I don't want to go inside. I physically resist going past the threshold. Someone behind me gives me a shove and holds my hand—my husband, probably—and we walk the long, center aisle to the front row. I don't make eye contact with anyone but can feel the weight of everyone's eyes on me. We sit directly in front of the casket and the giant poster of your face that's hanging on an easel. It's the photo from the inside of your book jacket where you're wearing your favorite blue hoodie, black T-shirt, and half smile. I remember when you sent me the proofs. I chose this one.

Then the service.

The eulogy.

The police escorts and the caravan to the cemetery.

The customary shoveling of the dirt into the hole.

The minyan that lasts until 10:00 p.m.

The *thank-you* and the *thank-you* and the *thank-you* and the *thank-you*.

The brutal exhaustion and the feeling that I very well might die, too.


The events of the following week are equally sad and surreal.

Like the unexpected feeling of betrayal when Leonard Nimoy dies the day after your funeral and your position of Tragic Dead Celebrity of the Week is usurped on social media.

The flying to Los Angeles two days after the funeral with Mom, Mike, and the baby. Dad refuses to go. He can't handle it.

The packing up of your house and your entire life, every knick-knack telling a story I'll never hear.

The endless stream of your wonderful friends lining up to help, comfort, feed, console, pack, and lean on.

The simultaneous elation and despair of the tribute shows.

The rehab journals from all three facilities and the overflowing folders of worksheets, suggested readings, and informational packets.

The sobriety chips and the copies of AA and NA in your backpack.

The drugs and the needles still in your bathroom drawer.

The things I wish I'd known, the things I knew but didn't say, the things I knew and said but should have said more.

The couch in the living room where you died that no one will sit on but me.

We gather in there one afternoon as Iris eats her afternoon snack. It's the time of day when sunlight pours through the curtains and paints everything in warmth. Surrounded by boxes, giant trash bags, and piles of things to *Give*, *Donate*, or *Keep*, I sit on the couch, while Mike and Mom sit on the floor. Iris wears a T-shirt that says *Oh Happy Day* and stands facing the couch, using it as a table for her crackers— a mix of water crackers and graham crackers. She has arranged them in a straight line. A few tiny bites in, she realizes that she has a round cracker in each hand but wants one of the square crackers in front of her. Instead of setting one of the crackers down and picking up another, she opts to bend at the waist and grab the cracker with her mouth like a little baby bird so now she has a cracker in each hand and one in her mouth.

"Oh, my god!" Mom cries.

All of us are immediately engulfed in laughter. Because she shares your comedic DNA, our positive feedback motivates her to do the bit again, and it lands even harder the second time. We quickly hit *can't breathe, tears pouring out of our eyes, falling on the floor* levels of laughter because here she is, this totally oblivious baby, eating graham crackers off a couch that a person died on a week before, which isn't at all funny but simultaneously so funny and exactly what we need.

It's the first of many times that Iris will save us from ourselves.

We spend one full week in LA, staying at your house with you not in it. Mike and I are literally sleeping in your bed. All I want is to go home and sleep in my *own* bed. Forever. But there's a baby, and the baby is sick with a cold, and I'm nervous for her to fly. If her ears get too clogged from the pressure, her eardrums could burst, which would be catastrophic for a baby who already has permanent hearing loss.

Armen was your best friend, favorite writing partner, and most prolific collaborator. He is having a tremendously hard time with all of this. His mom, who lives here in LA and came down to Houston for the funeral, has been endlessly helpful this week, so in the midst of the chaos, we ask her to arrange for an appointment with a local pediatrician. His office is cluttered with signed sports memorabilia. He writes Iris a prescription and gives us the green light to fly. Thank God. I can't deal with another fucking thing.

Packing up a person's life and clearing out someone else's fully lived-in house is no small feat. There are so many drawers to clean out and papers to shred. It's also physically painful.

My lower back aches.

My neck is locked into one position.

My jaw is tense.

My head is permanently migrained.

My ankle may be sprained. I keep walking into furniture. At one point, I run full speed into your bedpost and literally hit the ground, writhing in pain, unable to breathe.

Hitting the ground is a repeated theme of the grieving process.

The morning before we fly back home, the movers arrive to load up the truck and take your belongings back to Houston, where I will lock them in a storage facility down the street from our house until I have the mental capacity to figure out what to do with them. After the movers set out on their voyage, Mom and I embark on ours, driving the narrow, winding road into The Hills to meet with your therapist from sober living, where you'd been since the end of December. Once we finally reach the gate, we have to drive up another steep hill to get to the facility. It's so steep, I feel as though the car might roll backwards and we might fall off the mountainside to our deaths. As we make it to the top, I wonder if you ever made this drive while high. If so, man, were you functional.

Your therapist greets us warmly. He is a short, bald, rather slight and soft-spoken Indian gentleman with a melodic British accent and an unending supply of patience. I'm able to identify him immediately: a recovering heroin addict, nineteen years clean. You always talked about him as if he were a deity. This is exactly how I imagined him.

Once introductions are made, he and the owner of the facility escort us into one of the nearby cottages. It's a large, sun-drenched meeting room with giant windows and a wraparound porch with a view of lush hills and trees perched beside sprawling, expensive homes. There are plenty of comfortable couches and chairs scattered around the room. It feels cozy. The fireplace mantle is crowded with live plants. A modest flat-screen TV hangs on the wall in the corner. I wonder how many times you sat where I'm sitting now, staring at this tiny TV, wrestling with your choices, trying to figure out why the fuck you do what you do. And, now, here we are, trying to figure out why the fuck you did what you did.

Your therapist kindly and softly explains that the primary thing that kills addicts is the "just one more time" mentality. He's so gentle in his delivery. It's a tragic accident that no one intends. It's a waste. He explains that they had made special allowances for you to work off-site on Aziz Ansari's Netflix show, *Master of None*, while you were living here. This was unusual, but they felt like it would be a positive motivator. *Of course you manipulated them into this arrangement*, I think.

You were always an epic and infamous arguer with a penetrating ability to wear people down. I vividly remember the four-hour screaming match you had with your roommate in the Sherman Oaks house while I was visiting over whether a movie we'd just seen was good or bad. (It was *Funny Games*, and for the record, it *was* bad.) The fight started in the lobby of the theater, followed us into the car and, ultimately, moved into the house, where it continued all night. Your roommate literally threatened to move out.

The *Analyze Phish* podcast, where you tried to convince Scott Aukerman to like Phish, was the most Harris thing of all time because you were always obsessively determined to make people see things your way. Like Scott, I never liked the band Phish either because why would I, but for decades, you refused to accept this as a possibility. Once, when I was living in New York, you finally wore me down enough to get me to a show at Coney Island that you swore would change my life. Even though Jay-Z made a surprise cameo that night, it didn't. To you, this meant that there must be something wrong with me. I can still hear you say *Steph* in that way only you say that word with so much disappointment and aggravation.

Here's what we learn from your therapist: Ultimately, you wouldn't give up control. You wouldn't surrender and accept that you were powerless. Three times over the course of your seven-week stay, you refused a Vivitrol shot, a drug that would've made getting high impossible by blocking sensors in your brain for thirty days. And you fucking refused it. You weren't done. You had every intention of using again.

This was your third rehab over the course of one year *to the day* and the one we all thought would finally stick. You clearly needed something more long term; the thirty-day programs weren't cutting it. The first rehab was in Malibu. You checked in last year on my birthday, February 20, 2014. Despite the stellar reputation and $30,000 price tag, you relapsed immediately once you got out. Six months later, after you'd started shooting heroin, you checked into another thirty-day program in Oregon that proved to be equally ineffective.

This last (and final) rehab in Hollywood seemed like a great fit. It was close enough to home, so you could eventually integrate it into your life. You spoke highly of the people both in the program and running it. Plus, it was a longer commitment and would allow more time for the program to sink in and change you on a permanent, brain-chemistry kind of level. When you first got to The Hills at the tail end of December, you completed a thirty-day detox then moved to their sober living residence in February, where you were supposed to live for a period of months *at least*, before transitioning back into real life. But you only stayed in sober living for three weeks before checking yourself out.

We inquire about your mental state the day you checked out without telling us because you knew you'd be met with resistance. From our sporadic phone calls and emails, you sounded like you were doing well, and we wanted you to stay that way. We knew you would be moving to New York in two weeks to start shooting *Master of None* but hoped you'd stay in sober living until then. Any lapse in treatment could jeopardize your sobriety.

According to your therapist, you had your final session with him on Tuesday afternoon, February 17, right before checking out for good. You seemed perfectly fine, he explained. Totally sober. Nothing out of the ordinary. He had no reservations whatsoever about your transition back home.

You overdosed and died two days later.

Driving away from the Hills, I wonder why we even felt it necessary to visit. It wasn't going to bring you back. I suppose it's all part of the manic investigative phase, which is missing from the stages-of-grief flowchart. I keep trying to piece together a timeline, to crack the case, as if this will somehow soften the blow. I go over and over and over the facts like some deranged, sleep-deprived detective: You checked out of sober living on Tuesday afternoon. You booked your Airbnb for New York, where you would be heading in two weeks' time to start production on the Netflix series. The Airbnb tab was still open on your laptop. You did stand-up at Meltdown on Wednesday at 8:00 p.m. After the show, you came home. Or maybe you didn't come home. Maybe you went to Skid Row. Maybe you already had the drugs in your bathroom drawer or in the center console of your car.

Mom emailed you earlier that night about the *Parks and Recreation* series finale:

> So is each show going to say goodbye to the characters from here on out? I get the feeling this is how it's going to wrap up. It's very cute and sweet actually. Time to say goodbye. Hope you are on good footing still. I am very excited to see you. Are you nervous about living in NY? A great new adventure for you. I think you are up to the task. How is the house hunting going? Steph turns 34 on Friday BTW. Love you very much. Mom

You responded at 12:00 a.m. her time, 10:00 p.m. your time:

> There's only one more Parks episode left and it's the big
> farewell episode that will make you cry. i found a cool place
> to live in Manhattan. I feel good!! I am feeling very fortunate.
> Love you.

And you were found dead on Thursday around noon.

It doesn't make any sense. It will never make any sense. What happened between clicking send and sticking a needle in your arm?

I spend hours trying to figure it out, sifting through texts and emails, listening to voicemails, interrogating your friends. Nothing. There is nothing. There is nothing to figure out because there is no case to crack. You were an addict, and it was a stupid, senseless fucking accident. It's as tragically simple as that.

This random guy who lived with you at The Hills has messaged me several times about coming by your house to pick up some of his gear from your music room. Aside from his gear not being my priority at the moment, I don't know this person and am hesitant to invite him into your home to potentially steal your drum kit and whatever other fancy shit you have back there. In the midst of this whirlwind, I don't know how to gauge who's a legitimate friend and who's out to capitalize on your death. Your tragic story has been plastered all over the internet for two weeks. Everyone has something to say. One girl wrote a detailed piece that she shared all over Facebook chronicling the details of your sexual relationship. Our mother read it. Lots of people we've never heard of have reached out to Mom and me on Facebook to say how close you were, how much you meant to them, and how devastated they are that you're gone. It's a difficult thing to field, and I'm paranoid that people will take advantage of that.

I check with Paul and Michael, your bandmates from Don't Stop or We'll Die, and they confirm that you did, indeed, have a "Secret Rehab Band," so I give this guy the green light. He comes with a driver or chaperone or something—a Henry Rollins type. The bodyguard tells us six people from sober living have overdosed on heroin in the last nine months. Six people. Six daughters, sons, husbands, wives, sisters, brothers. Six other families have lived through this merciless nightmare. You knew the statistics but were convinced it wouldn't happen to you. I make shitty small talk with the guy from Secret Rehab Band, all the while resenting that he's alive and you're dead.

# 05
—
## Week Three

Once the house is packed up and the movers have come and gone and the rooms are empty, aside from a couple of beds, dressers, a dining room table, and the sofa in the living room, we say goodbye to your house in Los Feliz that we'll never see again and head back to LAX. We return the rental car and take the shuttle to the terminal, and as we sit at the gate, waiting for the plane to arrive, it hits me that we're flying back home to Houston, but I'm not ready to go back to my life.

I *can't* go back to my life.

It's March 7, and I haven't been to work since February 19. I text my boss to tell him I'm still a mess and currently have the baby's cold and possibly a sprained ankle (from the bedpost). I ask for more time. He tells me to take another week. One week plus spring break, which is the following week, will give me two more weeks. To do what? I don't know.

The grief takes up so much space that there's not much room for anything else. When I'm not thinking about how bleak life is going to be without you, I'm signing on some dotted line and trying my best to wake up every day for the sake of Iris. I force myself to smile in her presence because she's a loving, innocent baby who deserves a smiling mother. This is taking all the energy I have. As a result, my ability to think and remember is notably compromised. I frequently say one word but mean another. Constantly, I hear "You told me that already."

It's all choppy and messy and nonlinear. One emotion doesn't flow neatly into another; it hits me suddenly, like morning sickness, and can't be pushed down. The only way to make it stop is to vomit up the feeling—to feel it deeply and loudly. I cry and cry and cry. Then I'm suddenly making a joke: "If he wasn't already dead, I'd fucking kill him." And everyone laughs.

It comes and goes and comes and goes. You don't pass one stage, scratch it off the list, and graduate onto the next. It's not compartmentalized like the chart suggests. It's circuitous and never-ending. Joan Didion said it better: "Grief has no distance. Grief comes in waves, paroxysms, sudden apprehensions that weaken the knees and blind the eyes and obliterate the dailiness of life."

"Sudden apprehension" is pretty much the theme of daily life, once the perpetual sobbing subsides. No one (besides Joan Didion) talks about that. You hear about anger, denial, bargaining, acceptance, but never about the crippling anxiety. I'm already prone to anxiety, but it reaches a fever pitch after the initial shock wears off.

Once we get back to Houston, I begin to displace all my sorrow on anxiety over Iris's health. Every time I call her name, and she doesn't immediately turn around, I decide she's lost the rest of her hearing. Every time she gets a diaper rash, I assume it's the measles. I worry about everything, really. I worry when Mike walks the dog at night or when I drive with the baby in the car. I worry that something bad is lurking behind every corner or ready to fall from the sky. I worry, worry, worry. Even though I'm going to therapy two, sometimes three, times a week, I'm either sad or gearing up for the next shitstorm. It's exhausting. I just want to sleep. That's all I want to do. If I'm asleep, I can't worry or cry or think about how my only brother is dead. Plus, you are alive in my dreams. In my dreams, everything is as it was.

Here is what I am supposed to do:

I am supposed to tell funny stories about when we were kids at your rehearsal dinner.

I am supposed to look into your baby's eyes and see you reflected in them.

I am supposed to grow old with you by my side.

Here is what I am *not* supposed to do:

I am not supposed to tell funny stories at your funeral about when we were kids.

I am not supposed to sit on the ground, peering into a giant hole at a casket we chose for you from a brochure.

I am not supposed to wonder what you look like in there, wearing your favorite pajama pants and Phish T-shirt, holding a set of drumsticks.

The permanence of death is unbearable. I can't fix it. I can't make it better. I am powerless—the thing you could never quite accept. My inner victim is loud and self-pitying. *Why did my brother have to be a drug addict? Why did he have to die? Why do I have to live life from this point forward without him? Why is all of this happening* **to me**?

It all blurs together and feels like a punishment for some transgression in a past life. I feel like that tragic family that people reference in conversations to feel better about themselves.

It all feels so unfair.

I was five years old when Mom informed me that life wasn't fair. You were there. I saw the scene just the other day in an old home movie. In the wake of your death, I've been watching lots of them. It's a masochistic exercise. The ones in which you're a little baby, cooing and kicking your feet, laughing wildly when someone says *Boo!* are especially painful. The one where I wore a white tutu and married you and your friend Andrea in our living room when you were five years old is also a tearjerker.

Most of them are hilarious. Like the mock interview you did in the fifth grade with your best friend Ryan that quickly devolved into you taking off your clothes and mooning the camera. Or your ten-year-old karaoke birthday party, where you performed Mariah Carey's "Hero" at the top of your lungs. Or that Hanukkah when you got your favorite Michelangelo Teenage Mutant Ninja Turtles costume set, complete with nunchakus. On the tape, Dad calls you *Michael* and you quickly correct him in your tiny three-year-old voice: "Michelangelo!"

"Oh sorry, Michelangelo," Dad says.

There are piles of DVDs with which to torture myself. Mom has gone to great lengths over the years to organize them. It borders on mental illness. They're all labeled and dated neatly in black Sharpie. She's a former second-grade teacher, so her penmanship is Pinterest-worthy.

In this one home movie, you're two; I'm five. Dad is recording, as usual. Mom chimes in regularly off-camera. You're standing in the breakfast room of our old house on Yarwell, shaggy-haired and tiny, holding a big, red plastic bat in one hand and an inflated pink ball with stars all over it in the other.

"Okay," Dad says as he focuses the camera on you. "You're on TV now. Harris, you ready to play ball?"

I take the bat out of your hands and stand inches in front of you.

"Give him the bat, Stephanie," Dad demands.

I hold my ground. "No!"

"Let him have it first, then you're next," Mom says as she takes it out of my hands and gives it back to you.

I scream as if someone has set me on fire, then cry and collapse, face down, into the couch.

No one seems to care.

"Harris, you ready to play ball?" Dad asks. "Let's play ball!"

Within moments, I am on my feet and creeping back into the shot.

"Move, Stephanie. Stephanie. Move." Mom demands, audibly annoyed.

"Ready, Harris?" Dad is still trying to get you in the zone. He doesn't yet know that you will never really be into it, that a couple years later, when he's coaching your Little League team, you will pick flowers in the outfield during baseball games like Ferdinand the Bull.

"Me!" you shout. "My bah!"

By this point, I have taken the bat again and am standing right behind you, ready to swing hard into your head.

"Harris, move," Mom says. "She's gonna hit you with that bat."

You turn toward me and reach for the bat that I hold high over my head, so you can't reach it. (It's really the only time in my life this

37

tactic worked for me. As an adult, I stand at barely five feet.) You scream in frustration and scratch my upper arm.

"*Ow!*" I shout and drop the bat. I swat you back on the arm.

You are unfazed. Rather, you grab the fallen bat, run right up to the camera, and smile. You are proud of yourself for getting the bat and winning a round. Dad finally throws the ball to you. You swing.

"Pway bah!" you say with enthusiasm.

"That's not fair," I whine.

"Nobody said life is fair, Stephanie," Mom says. "You'll learn that soon enough."

## 06

—

## One Month

Even time moves differently now.

It used to be measured in minutes, hours, days, weeks, and months. Now, it's measured before you died and after. It feels like yesterday and a hundred years ago all at the same time. It feels like I want to burn something to the ground and do nothing forever.

Going back to work is terrifying. I don't know how I will form words, much less inspire the gifted and talented youth of America where you and I once went to high school together. It's a demanding and rewarding job that's often emotionally draining and requires me to be fully present. But I'm not. I also don't give a shit about theater anymore. Or anything, for that matter.

I carry one of your sobriety chips in my pocket that whole first week back. It reads:

> *God grant me the serenity to accept the things I cannot change,*
> *The courage to change the things I can,*
> *And the wisdom to know the difference.*

An impossible task.

Ninety-nine percent of the time, I feel like some sort of alien—seemingly human and going through the motions but from another galaxy altogether and unfamiliar with the ways of this world. And no one here can win. I feel angry when people don't acknowledge the situation, and I feel angry when they inevitably say the wrong thing. *How are you?* feels like an act of violence.

Social media continues to be a sharp and swift form of torture. So many new babies, engagement announcements, and wedding photos. So many people living perfect, unscathed little lives. As ambivalent as I was about your death being a trending topic, I remember how empty I felt when everyone seemed to forget about you a week or so later and went back to bitching about traffic, sharing YouTube videos, and posting photos of their dinners. Nothing makes the pain worse than seeing that everyone else is able to move on. I think: *People are the worst.* And then I think how you would tell me they mean well. And they do. They really do.

They bring food.

They call to check in.

They keep calling when I don't respond.

They send beautiful, thoughtful cards and messages.

They donate money to your scholarship fund.

They offer to help with Iris and groceries and life in general.

They let me take my time returning to the fold.

They shower me with love.

It helps.

## 07

—

## Before

### June 2013

After our wedding, my new husband and I barreled headfirst into *real life*. Engaged in December, married in March, and pregnant in May. I took the pregnancy test after drinking six shots of sake at a work happy hour. Aside from the guilt I felt about drinking while pregnant and the sheer shock that it happened so fast, the news was glorious.

The last week in June, I chaperoned an annual school trip with my high school students. I was taking them to a thespian festival at the University of Nebraska. It was right at the end of my first trimester, which meant I couldn't tell anyone yet why I was exhausted, cranky, starving, and in a tizzy about the X-ray machine at the airport. I also had a notably bad summer cold and spent my downtime lying on a stone mattress in a tiny dorm room, Googling articles about the side effects of Sudafed on fetuses.

In the midst of my internet-forum binge, Harris called to tell me he broke up with his girlfriend. I was deeply confused. We all thought she was the One. *He* thought she was the One. They seemed to be a perfect fit, especially in juxtaposition to the last two serious relationships. Not because he chose terrible partners. Quite the opposite.

The women he dated were stellar. It's just that Harris had a pattern of falling head over heels in love then eventually losing interest and calling it off; then once she moved on, he'd regain interest and beg her to come back only to lose interest again or be cheated on because she was over it; and then, fueled by jealousy and rage, he would want her back more than ever before. The cycle was maddening.

But it wasn't like that with Sarah. With her, it all seemed effortless and meant to be. She quickly became part of the family. When we'd spent Thanksgiving at Harris's house in LA six months earlier, she'd made homemade chopped liver and helped my mom in the kitchen. She was easygoing and funny and weird in a good way and notably pleasant to be around. She looked at him with such adoration. I remember when he first told me about her in Vegas while we were on a family vacation the previous summer. She was the first thing that came out of his mouth when he saw me at the hotel check-in counter. I don't even think he said hello before diving into details about this amazing girl he'd met at a party the night before. Yet here he was a year later telling me the "spark was gone." He was too young to be tethered to one person. He wanted to explore his options and see what else was out there.

I assumed this meant she was getting in the way of his drug use. Even though he was a twenty-eight-year-old boy-man living in a saturated land of beautiful people, it was such a sudden and unexpected change of heart that no other explanation made sense.

I asked about the pills. He said he had been going to some outpatient detox place and was taking Suboxone. Their breakup had nothing to do with the pills; he just viewed her as a friend now; the passion was gone, fucking *blah, blah, blah, bullshit, bullshit, blah, blah, blah*. I didn't believe a word he said. Ever since he told me he was an addict and forced me to stay quiet about it, I felt like someone had hijacked my brother and replaced him with a secret evil-twin version. He'd been lying about his drug habit for who knows how long before he told me. What else was he lying about? And who the fuck tells his sister he's a drug addict three days before her wedding? An asshole. My real brother wasn't an asshole. *This* guy was an asshole.

A week or so later, I got a desperate email from the girlfriend/ex-girlfriend. Not quite sure where they stood at this point:

> If someone doesn't step in now, he's going to die. This is
> very very serious now and can't wait any longer. Please help
> him and maybe tell your mom and dad. He doesn't tell peo-
> ple the real truth and severity of it. It is deadly serious now.
> I'm so sorry but he is doing himself in and I had to share
> this with you.

Not exactly subtle. At this point, I was three months pregnant, and the stress was a room with no air. Between Harris's secret and the baby I was carrying, there wasn't any room left inside of my body. Something had to come out. She literally said he was "going to die." How could I live with myself if she was right? I had to tell my parents. This is how I justified my betrayal.

It finally happened at my parents' annual Fourth of July party. My best friend, Chloe, was there, and she kept insisting that I tell them. And I wanted to, I *really* did, but I was terrified of losing his trust. Later that night, after all the other guests had gone home, Chloe and I were lying on the couch in food comas, whispering about the Harris situation. My mom pried like she did when we were ten years old, giggling in the backseat of her minivan: "What's going on over there, girls?" Chloe and I made eye contact, and her eyes said it again: *You have to tell them.*

"Ugh, I have to tell you something terrible," I blurted out.

"What? What's the matter?" my mom asked, concerned.

Their faces froze. This isn't a sentence you want to hear from your pregnant daughter.

"Harris is a drug addict. He told me right before the wedding and made me swear I wouldn't tell you and told me he was gonna handle it, but I keep getting these panicked emails from Sarah, and she's really worried about him, and I don't know what to do. I'm worried he's gonna do something stupid or kill himself or something fucked up and you have to help."

I could see them instantly sucked into quicksand, although they managed to remain relatively calm. No tears or hysterics. They absorbed the information and tried to formulate a plan. Coincidentally, they were visiting Harris in LA in a few weeks and, given the weight of this news, they decided a face-to-face conversation with him would be most effective. They'd figure out what needed to be done. Action steps. Crisis/solution. The problem would be solved.

"Steph, take it off your plate," my mom said. "We will handle this."

This felt like telling my feet to stop swelling. Impossible.

Life with an addict means constantly revising the script. The story is always changing—and quickly. A few days after the panic-stricken Fourth of July emails, we got an unexpected update from Sarah:

> I just wanted to let you know that Harris is being very sweet
> and loving again, and he's decided to get some help to get
> clean. He has an appointment with a great Dr. tomorrow to

discuss doing an outpatient program. It'll help him to have a professional get him the right supplements he needs, and to help him come off easily I think. I can keep you updated but I just wanted you to know that he's being so good now and I think everything is going to be fine.

So, good news? Temporary good news? Death was off the table? Off the table for now? It was difficult to keep the story straight across multiple state lines. He was in therapy, then he was out. He was doing an outpatient program, then he wasn't. He was on Suboxone, then he was off. He was back with his girlfriend, then they broke up. Then they were just friends. Then they were full-blown enemies. He obsessed over her regardless. He was a very obsessive human being in general. In fairness, so am I. Perhaps it's genetic.

During this time, I tried to temper my tone, to stay calm and supportive, to mask much of my frustration. For one, he didn't know that Sarah was sending us updates, and I didn't want to betray my source. And two, he was acting so erratic that I didn't want to cause more stress and push him further over the edge.

My mom and I constantly compared notes:

*Have you heard from Harris this week?*

*Did Harris text you today?*

*Any word from Harris?*

*Any further communication from Harris?*

*Harris anxiety* became a defining characteristic of our family dynamic. Mostly, we were in the dark and disconnected from his day to day. Plus, having a demanding job was a great front for his addiction. Work was always the perfect excuse for not responding to my texts for days, for why he'd been out of touch, for why he seemed extra prickly.

Despite the false alarm from Sarah that Harris was on the mend, their relationship continued to deteriorate over the next several months and, eventually, seemed just as dysfunctional as the others. The making up and breaking up reached a boiling point in late November, when Harris sent her a series of exceptionally bleak emails that said stuff like, "I was sober and I did it with hopes of us being together again, and now I'm a suicidal junkie and it's your fault." And: "When I die, which is hopefully soon from pills (I tried last night but woke up somehow), it's entirely your fault." And: "You look my parents in the eye at the funeral and tell them all i asked was to talk to you and you refused." And: "Actually picture what you would feel like and how you could've prevented it. Remember this moment." And: "I loved you."

My mom and I knew about the emails because she forwarded them to us and urged us *again* to intervene but said it with less patience this time. She was clearly done. She copied her dad on the emails, who responded with similar sentiments. They were *all* done. He needed help. Bottom line. Couldn't be any clearer.

But there was a significant obstacle: Harris was a grown, financially self-sufficient man who was living 1,500 miles away. There was no rock bottom in this story. My parents couldn't cut him off and put him on the streets until he got the help he needed. He had a great job, a beautiful home, a stable income, and a stellar reputation. He got up every day and went to work at a job everyone would kill for. He was a prolific comedy podcaster and continued to get hired for more and more writing jobs. He was working on a project with Scott Rudin. He had an assistant who took care of the details. We were worried about the drug use, but from the outside looking in, this was a person who appeared to be extremely on top of his shit. What were we supposed to do with this sort of addict? How could we get him the help he needed?

At a loss, my mom forwarded the emails to Harris and cc'd me, asking him why he couldn't just get out of their lives. He, of course, had a very simple explanation that completely evaded the issue: "I tried to get her attention and it worked too well and now we are here." *This* was his explanation. He was just trying to "get her attention." I mean, what the fuck.

Our correspondence continued like this for a while. I asked, "Can you just stop talking to her?" I reiterated that she and her *entire* family had been very clear that they didn't want him in their lives for a dozen reasons.

My mom was more direct. "Stop contacting her in any manner. It sounds to me like their next step is to hire a lawyer to keep you away from her and that means lots of trouble for you. They cannot be any clearer about wanting you out of their lives. Please hear them! Enough Harris!"

Harris said this was like a movie where people were trying to trick him into being crazy and that it had all been blown way out of proportion. "If people are trying to make you sound crazy," my mom asked, "why are you making it easy for them to think that about you?"

He couldn't accept that he might be at fault, that he'd finally pushed it too far, and the game was over. It was a sobering moment for all of us. All of us except Harris.

Back in Houston, Mike and I bought a tiny, one-hundred-year-old bungalow in a charming neighborhood, right across the street from a big park that was always packed with children. It was all very picture-perfect. I continued to displace my anxiety about drug addiction and impending motherhood on an obsessive online search for the perfect nursery wallpaper. The internet is full of wallpaper, so the task was all-consuming for many weeks, and I welcomed the distraction. It was as if my subconscious decided that if I could just find the right wallpaper, everything would be okay.

Harris flew home for Thanksgiving and Christmas, as usual. We mainly overate and watched the stack of DVDs he'd been sent to screen before awards season. He was consumed with writing a pilot for NBC (that ultimately got rejected) about the relationship between this lovable, twenty-eight-year-old burnout who loves Phish and lives in his parents' basement and his brilliant fourteen-year-old brother who invented and made millions off Cone Tips, the chocolatey bottom of a Drumstick ice-cream cone, which was one of Harris's favorite things to eat since childhood. He was notably stressed, low-grade grumpy, and furiously finger-pecking away on his laptop around the clock.

From the time he told me he had a problem with pills in March 2013 to the time he checked into rehab for the first time in February 2014, there was so much going on in my life that it was hard to fully comprehend what was happening in his. In the span of one year, I had gotten engaged, married, and pregnant. I changed my legal identity from Wittels to Wachs. We bought and moved into our first home. I had a doctor's appointment at least once a week. I had to put together a baby registry. And what I knew—*what I believed*—was that Harris was busy with work, in therapy, and trying to stay sober.

## 08
—

## Two Months

Visiting the cemetery isn't a natural urge, but the day before your birthday I force myself to go. It's the first time I've been here since the funeral. It's also April 19, the two-month anniversary of your death. The grass hasn't even taken root. With tear-streaked cheeks I sit there for a while, in front of your temporary gravesite marker, then walk around to meet your neighbors. I'm particularly drawn to the ones who died young. The tragedies. I come back and sit a while longer but soon become weirded out by all the roly polies crawling around in the grass. There are just so many. It's like that scene in *Lost Boys* with the maggots in the Chinese food. You loved that movie. I wonder how you feel about roly polies.

For the duration of my life, I will wonder how you feel about all sorts of things.

Like:

Doesn't Bob Durst remind you of Dad a little bit?

Do you think the guy from *The Staircase* killed his wife?

Did you ever make that pasta dish that Jon Favreau made Scarlett Johansson in *Chef*? The recipe was listed online.

How fucked-up is it that they didn't just choose *one* Bachelorette? Bullshit.

What does that guy on Facebook that we both know do for work? Like, how does he live in the world?

Do you think when people say they will pray for you that they actually pray for you or is it just a figure of speech?

Before taking off, I play you all of Iris's latest videos.

Like the one of her wiping her own nose on command.

And the one of her chasing the dog around the house naked.

And the one of her listening to a record for the first time: George Harrison's *All Things Must Pass*.

I would be lying right here beside you by now if it weren't for her.

## 09

—

## Before

### January 2014

On January 21, 2014, at 12:17 p.m., I gave birth to a magical creature from the Universe of All of My Hopes and Dreams. A daughter: Iris Phoebe. I felt a tugging and a pulling and then the relief of that piercing cry as the doctor raised her high above the blue C-section curtain like Simba from *The Lion King*. "The Circle of Life" could have underscored the entire scene. It was the closest I'd ever come to some sort of spiritual nirvana. A catharsis. Mike gasped loudly and exploded into tears of joy. I gasped loudly and exploded into tears of joy. The baby shrieked with all the force her little lungs could muster. The nurses wrapped her up in her sweet little blanket, and Mike carried her over to me, laying her warm, tiny body in my arms. She immediately started sucking on my finger for comfort. The sweetest thing. She was finally here—so real, so small, so beautiful.

It was a perfect moment in time.

A couple of weeks later, sleep-starved and running on empty, we sat in an audiologist's office, our two-week-old daughter hooked up to a host of wires and electrodes, and heard fragments of the shocking diagnosis that would permanently change our lives: "Iris was born with a mild sensorineural hearing loss in both ears…one in a thousand babies…needs hearing aids as soon as possible…will wear them for the rest of her life…no cure" and some other stuff about the dozens of tests we'd need to do to figure out the cause.

I had no idea what any of this meant but was devastated all the same. Something was "wrong" with our baby, and I couldn't interpret it into news that made any sense. No one on either side of our families had hearing loss. Both my grandmothers lived into their nineties with totally functional ears. I had a healthy pregnancy with numerous ultrasounds. I followed all the rules and honored the restrictions. I didn't eat sushi or take the Sudafed. I did everything right, and this happened anyway.

While I sat there sobbing, I heard another family through the thin wall next door who had obviously brought in their two-week-old for her follow-up hearing screening, too. I heard the mother cheer, "Yay! Good job! You did it!" I heard them all laugh and celebrate and thank the nurse who administered the test. I heard them leave the office and imagined them walking out of the hospital, getting into their car, and driving back to their normal lives as normal new parents of a newborn baby with normal hearing.

Before sending us on our way, the audiologist handed us a fat packet with all sorts of data on how children with hearing loss inevitably fail at life in countless ways. Only two weeks old and already at risk of falling behind socially, emotionally, and academically, of being depressed, alienated, and possibly even suicidal someday.

This wasn't the movie I'd directed in my mind. That movie starred a radiant postpartum mother and her perfect newborn baby: Mom taking a brisk walk every morning with her baby tucked tightly in her gender-neutral stroller under layers of soft blankets or nuzzled close to Mom in her organic baby sling as passers-by *ooh* and *aah* over her beauty, sharing frequent play dates with friends who also have little ones, commiserating over poopy diapers and sleep deprivation, writing funny anecdotes in a handmade baby book from Etsy, lying in bed with the perfect little family, daydreaming about who she'll be when she grows up.

While I adored my precious baby and had been fiercely attached to her from the start, I didn't want to get out of bed or go on a brisk walk. I didn't have any funny anecdotes in me. I didn't want to see anyone. I resented the fact that my friends with "normal" children had luxury worries like baby acne, diaper rash, and cradle cap. I felt angry and bitter that this only happens to three in one thousand babies, and it was happening to her, and I was consumed with anxiety about the impending genetics test, kidney ultrasound, eye exam, CMV, EEG, MRI, ABR. Never before had letters been so scary. I was mourning the loss of the perfect life I'd dreamed up. I suddenly had a child with a permanent disability and was terrified about what it meant for her future.

Mike, on the other hand, had been taking it in stride from the beginning. When she didn't pass her newborn hearing screening at the hospital, he simply said, "She'll just get a cochlear implant or something." I was on the other end of the spectrum, spending most of my days and never-ending nights with a baby attached to my bleeding nipples, crying uncontrollably, compulsively Googling articles about hearing loss and related genetic diseases and typing a laundry list of questions for doctors and specialists in my iPhone Notes:

Will she need speech therapy?
Will her voice be affected?

How do hearing aids work? Is it like normal hearing or does it
sound weird?

Will she be able to hear birds chirping? Whispering?

Can we raise our voices or will it be too loud?

Concerts, music classes, dance classes, movie theaters, airplanes?

Crowds/group conversations—hard to hear?

Can she hear us if we call for her from the other room?

Do we have to be looking at her when we talk?

Background noise distracting?

Mainstream school or special ed?

Does she wear them all the time? Bedtime? Shower? Swimming?

What can she hear now?

Everything was unknown. I felt so powerless.

Fifteen hundred miles away, my brother was waging a similar war with
himself. It had been almost a year since he told me he was a drug
addict, and it was becoming harder and harder for him to manage
his life behind the scenes. His on-and-off-Suboxone, in-and-out-of-
therapy approach to sobriety wasn't working anymore, and his therapist finally said he had to go to actual rehab in order to get *actual*
sober. Harris, however, still had a collection of excuses about why he
couldn't go, chief among them work work work work work work work
work work work work work work work work work work work work work
work work work work work work work work work work work work work
work work work work work work work work work work work work work

work work work work work work work work work work work work work work work work. (Lies.)

A week after we received the hearing loss diagnosis, my brother booked a flight home to meet his three-week-old niece. He also agreed to start *actual* rehab once he got back to LA. His plan was to come home, meet the baby, get in some family time, fly back to LA, and check himself into rehab. It was a monumental step, and we were gushing with support. We figured if he could just get there, the problem would be solved. A happy ending was on the horizon.

Harris walked into my house at 8:00 p.m. wearing his signature baggy jeans, white T-shirt, blue hoodie, and black North Face backpack. I assaulted him with a bear hug. He was home. He was safe. He was going to get sober. Seeing him in the flesh gave me a momentary break from my despair, although the scent of stale smoke that accompanied him into every room was especially potent to my postpartum nose. I was acutely aware that he would be holding my new baby in a moment, smelling like he was recently set on fire.

He took the baby, awkwardly at first, not knowing where to put his hands for proper support but became more comfortable after a few moments. I could see his spirit lift as he took her in. I could see that he loved her already. She was already validating his decision to get help. He stared with wonder into the eyes of his niece, into all that innocence and hope and promise, and said, "Hi, I'm Uncle Harris." My heart bounced around in my chest like a pinball.

Over the next few days, Harris set up camp on the couch with Iris. She slept on his chest for hours at a time, and he was at peace with her there. It was good to have him home, even though I cried through most of his visit. It wasn't even crying, really. It was just this sort of constant leaking out of my eyes.

"This is the most depressed I've ever seen you," Harris said one day, holding Iris on the couch during one of her napping jags. "Steph, this will always be normal for her," he said matter-of-factly. "She'll never know any different. And then she'll get her hearing aids, and those will be normal, too. She's not carrying a heavy burden. She's just a chill baby who wants to be a baby. This is hard on *you*—not *her*." Such a simple notion, but those are often the ones that ring most true and something my brother was always good for. And I needed to hear it. I still felt like shit, but I filed his sentiments away and pulled them out often in the future for review.

Harris researched a variety of upscale rehab facilities while he was home. They all looked like spas and employed professional chefs. The one he finally chose in Malibu had a long history of celebrity clientele. He had terrific insurance that would cover his stay, but as a frame of reference thirty days at this place *without insurance* would literally cost more than I made in three years as a public-school teacher. But this is how Harris did things: excessively and to the extreme.

I trace this behavior back to childhood. When we were kids, my mom would turn Harris loose inside the grocery store with his own cart, allowing him to fill it to the brim with whatever sugary garbage he could find. Once, when he was six, we went to a Ruth's Chris Steak House for someone's birthday. Grandma (Dad's mom) and Ganny (Mom's mom) were both there. Harris wanted lobster, and Grandma told him to go pick the one he wanted from the tank, while Ganny shook her head in exasperation. Naturally, Harris picked the biggest one. This poor lobster was over five pounds. The waiter came over to the table clutching the squirming crustacean between his metal tongs. "This is a $150 lobster," he said, certain an adult would intervene and say, "Please put that beast back in the tank. Our apologies. His eyes are bigger than his stomach." But that didn't happen. "Of course, he can have it!" Grandma exclaimed. So, Harris got the $150 lobster and learned that the finer things in life could easily be had. I think he ate two bites.

As an adult, this tendency toward overindulgence continued. I was eight months pregnant when he came home for Christmas a few months earlier, and we drove an hour outside of town to a highly-rated-on-Yelp steak house for my mom's birthday. Harris insisted we order the authentic Japanese Wagyu four-ounce filet mignon from Kagoshima Prefecture for $100 even though nobody wanted it but him *because it cost $100 for four ounces of meat.* He wanted this dish *in addition* to our entrees, as an appetizer of which we could all take a single bite: a $25 bite. I, of course, said this was an absurd waste of money, but he argued that if you have the opportunity to experience something for the first time, why not do it regardless of the cost? Money wasn't money to my brother like money is money for normal people; it was merely a thing you needed to experience life to the fullest.

This isn't to say that everything he owned was gilded and covered in diamonds. Quite the opposite. While he enjoyed expensive multicourse meals, his true love was fast food. He appreciated cinematic master-pieces but DVR'd every season of *The Bachelor.* He had a professionally decorated home, yet a pink bottle of Mr. Bubble was always perched on the side of his bathtub. This was Harris. He did life in his own unique way and was as complicated and contradictory as they come.

Since he had the money, Harris decided to splurge and spend it on the finest of rehabs, and we were confident that his thirty-day luxury hiatus would fix whatever bug had lodged itself inside of him. It had to. Because despite outward appearances, his pilot light was off. Even though Harris was always surrounded by friends and made fun and funny a guiding priority in his life, he struggled with sadness. In public, he was still everything that made him, him: gregarious, funny, charming, outgoing. But over the last year with the back pain and the pills and the on and off with the girlfriend, he'd become more detached and distant from us. His energy for conversation was either ephemeral or absent. When we were together as a family, we'd find ourselves firing off a zillion questions about the goings-on of his life but would get very little in return. Lots of "yes" or "no," and virtually no reciprocal questions. It often felt like talking to a teenager, frustrating and even hurtful at times. I justified his behavior by reasoning that maybe he just needed to shut down and reboot when he came home. He felt comfortable enough to not have to be "Harris" around us. He had so much success in such a short time at such a young age—maybe it was just too much.

Rehab was the solution, the cure-all that would resurrect him from the living dead. Even my dad, the medical professional who wrote actual textbooks, was certain this would do the trick. The thirty days would conflict with Iris's baby naming, which sucked, but we had to act fast on his willingness to go to treatment. Getting sober would make all sorts of future family events possible. It would keep him alive. We would just lie to everyone and say he had a work commitment. Easy.

I hugged him tightly before he headed back to LA. Although I was stranded in my own canyon of sadness, it had been comforting to look up and see my brother sitting there with me over the last few days. I was relieved he was finally willing to take action and confident it would work. Harris was a golden boy. He could do anything.

# 10

## Three Months

I just want somebody to tell me what the fuck happened the night you died. I want some fucking answers. When did you decide to use? Did you plan it all day, like right before breakfast, or was it a last-minute moment of weakness? Did you have any second thoughts or did you just plunge right in? What happened right before you did it? Who did you talk to? Had you relapsed prior to leaving sober living or did it happen after you got out on Tuesday? This question plagues me the most.

I go to the storage unit to drop off some baby stuff. Baby stuff takes up so much room—it's astounding. The last, and only other, time I was here was to open it up for the movers when they arrived from LA. The halls are still and quiet. I think: *This would be an effective place to commit a murder.* The motion lights click on as I turn each corner of the winding hallway. Row after row of boxes stuffed with people's shit. I open the heavy, metal garage door, breathe in, and sob. Sometimes if I inhale too deeply, it pushes some internal button and tears come pouring out of my face when I exhale. It happens all the time. Having a conversation with the pediatrician. Checking out at the grocery store. Opening the big garage door to a storage unit. Looking at all your furniture and boxes full of hoodies and cool artwork crammed into a ten-by-ten-foot, climate-controlled box.

Lying in bed that night, binge-watching *Parenthood* and feeling sorry for myself that I'll never have a big family like these fictional characters on this television show, I remember that your cell phone has been sitting in the drawer of my bedside table, untouched, since we unpacked from our trip to LA over two months ago. I plug it in, and it's so dead that it takes several moments to wake up. Like coming out of a coma. The Apple logo flashes on the screen, followed by your favorite picture of Iris in her pink, animal-print footie pajamas sitting on her little pink chair with *Iris* embroidered on the back. She is looking directly at the camera with a look on her face that says *Enough with the pictures already, lady*. It feels like I'm powering up a portal to another dimension.

I open the Notes app and scroll through your brain, some complete—but mostly incomplete—set lists, thoughts, jokes, ideas. The set from your last show at Meltdown the night you died is at the top:

> I tell ya, I walk around this city now and I don't know what is and what isn't a banksy. That's exactly what banksy wants.
>
> Vampires can't die unless their heart is stopped. But like, same with humans? just havin some fun with thought experiments, iono
>
> It always kinda bums me out when I see a band play a show and none of them have on a wedding ring.
>
> If conservative idiots consider life to begin at conception, then why do they all celebrate their birthdays as the day they were born?
>
> I'll never not be surprised at how far back the vagina is.

Genuinely enjoy Keith and Harry Connick's banter. Great guys with fun tudes.

When a car starts going a little before the light turns green, Im like "oh shit they've been to this intersection before." I like that move.

I wonder what vibe I carry when I walk into a room. Lord I hope it's chill.

2 legitimately 2 quitimately

I'll never be at 69 followers again. Wait! UNLESS I say the n-word a bunch of times and LOSE enough followers!… but is it worth it…?

You hear about the fat guy who created a dramedy? He got an Emmy nom nom nom.

Serious question: If you could suck your own dick, would you cum in your mouth? I think I'd try to finish on my tits.

In trailers, I love when they cut right in the middle of someone saying "motherfucker." Hell yea I'm gonna see it! Gotta see if they say it!

I had AIDS once

Aw man, when eye boogers turn sharp, forget about it

Instagram's good for seein what people are up to.

Bummed I never tried white rice with barbecue sauce when I was making poverty meals in college.

I looove lettin someone else handle the small talk on an elevator when a new guy gets on. Prob my biggest passion.

Sorry to bum you out, but those two otters that held hands broke up and don't even speak anymore. There's kids too. It's a whole mess.

When two people have the same birthday that shit is crazy and deserves to be both noted and freaked out about.

To reiterate, when not one but TWO people share a birthday, for my money, doesn't get any more insane than that.

I just blew a 0.28. His name was Frank.

Waldo asked me to spot him at the gym. Couldn't do it.

When I search for something obscure, I feel bad for making my computer "work hard." Then I remember it's a computer. Then I give it a raise.

Wheat thins

Egg basket

Freud

Therapist inward and I was like you dont have to censor yourself, dawg! I'm chill!

Frozen dinners over how much wattage of microwave

Wish I was gay

Dentist

Scaffolding

Mcdonalds Taco Bell

OxyContin poisoning

Orange hair old guy

Google car pigeons

Lohan doc

That guy Plutonium

Jerk off high school hook ups

Lizard escape dog Harriet Tubman

I hate smoking sections unless we are talking about the movie the mask with Jim Carrey. The smoking section is my favorite part.

Pineapple cum

I can hear you saying each and every word in my head so clearly, inflection and all. It's comforting to hear your voice. *Also this*: "I just blew a 0.28. His name was Frank." So good, Harris. I mean, *truly good*.

I close the Notes app and stare at the screen, hoping to conjure up more of you. The little green phone icon catches my eye, and it hits me that I never checked your outgoing call log. *How did I miss that?* It's like one of those detective shows where the case is closed and the innocent guy is locked up for life without parole, but there's a tiny clue stuck under the cushion of the couch that the dog digs up and starts chewing on and, all of a sudden, everything finally makes sense and the detective realizes he had it all wrong.

You didn't check out of sober living until February 17, but looking at your call log, I see you called your dealer on February 10. Your friends mentioned his name when we were in LA after the funeral, and I recognized it immediately—it's not a common name. I know the rehab had been allowing you to come and go freely to work on *Master of None,* so barring the possibility of an afternoon coffee date with your dealer, I conclude that you'd been using heroin for an entire week before checking yourself out.

I get out of bed and head to the box containing the rehab journals and worksheets that I couldn't fully comprehend the week we cleaned out your house. I thumb through the pages and discover that you relapsed the day you got out of rehab *each* time you got out of rehab. But this time, it appears you'd relapsed a full seven days before you got out.

No one could have saved you. Not a girl. Not a sponsor. Not a mother or a father. Not a sister.

No one.

# 11

—

## Before

### February 2014

Harris finally went to rehab the day before Iris turned one month old, nearly a year to the day before he died. It was also my thirty-third birthday, but I wasn't feeling particularly festive. My baby had permanent hearing loss, my brother was in rehab, my nipples were cracked, and my body was starved for sleep. Still, Mike gave me a card. He's great at cards. This one had two little porcupines on the cover, giving each other Eskimo kisses. Inside were a few lottery tickets and a note that said:

*My love: Well everything seems to be going perfectly to plan—PSYCHE! While the past few weeks have been—at times—chaotic, sad, stupefying, depressing, unrelenting, and unfortunate—in the big scheme of things they have been wonderful: we started our family in earnest and got one beautiful child whose future is much brighter than the din of our recent moods would suggest. It might be right to say that this is a real "It was the best of times; it was the worst of times" moment in our lives. And while it is hard, there is no one else I can imagine who I'd rather have these "worst of times" with; or best of times. In light of our recent hardships, I've decided to put my faith in lotto games to turn our luck around. Knowing how the past weeks have gone, there is a small chance I chose the scratcher game where you end up having to pay the lottery commission. Take caution. Love You, Husband*

I sat with him on the edge of the bed as I read his beautiful words then cried into his shoulder.

Later that afternoon, Mike, my mom, and I toured the Center for Hearing and Speech, the place where, a year later, I'd get a call while changing the baby's diaper that would cause me to fall to the ground and pound the floor. I don't know it at the time, but this is the place where my life would forever change.

The center was great. It had a dedicated preschool for kids who were deaf and hard of hearing, audiologists and speech therapists, and you didn't even have to pay for parking, which was really the biggest selling point for us. It was my first glimmer of hope since the baby was born. This is where we need to be, I thought. We scheduled Iris for her first speech therapy session at five weeks old. I wasn't sure what an infant could really *do* in speech therapy, but they said it was critical, so we complied.

Harris wasn't allowed to use his cell phone at rehab—no texting, social media, or private phone calls—but he could call us from their landline and email freely. So, the next day I emailed him a photo of Iris posing for the one-month photo that I posted on Facebook. I'd propped her up on an armchair wearing a onesie with cupcakes all over it and snapped the photo before she toppled over.

**Subject: Iris is one month old today!**

And she loves you and is very proud of you. Xoxo

He responded:

she's cuuuute!! thanks for writing. write often if you can. I
don't have much other connection to the outside world. I
heard you're living with mom and dad. iris probably doesn't
care where she is, so whatevs.
    love,
    uncle harris

Good news: He was still funny!

Bad news: We had been displaced to my parents' two-bedroom
condo with a newborn baby. And a dog. And a bassinet and a baby tub
and a bouncer and diapers and wipes and various creams and hearing-
aid accessories and ample changes of clothes for daily blowouts and a
suitcase full of favorite books and toys. The day after Harris flew back
to LA, I found mushrooms growing out of the carpet in the baby's
room—in the home we'd purchased just five months before. Once
they tore out the sheetrock to get to the toxic poison, the house was
rendered uninhabitable, especially with a baby in the mix.

If this was fiction, and I was the author, I'd think it sounded
too far-fetched to be believable. Yet there we were. At my mom's.
Indefinitely. I was starting to understand that I'm not in charge and
nothing is in my control.

Iris got fit for her first pair of hearing aids a few days later. I
emailed Harris another photo of her, this time with pink bubble-gum

putty stuck in her ears. I told him how terrible it was to watch. She was so mad—screaming, crying, and bright red. I told him my doctor put me on Zoloft, albeit a small dose because of the breastfeeding. I'd gone in for a routine checkup and they gave me this 32-question test on an iPad to determine whether I had postpartum depression. The test concluded that I was a fucking mess. I hoped the meds would help. I needed them to help. I told Harris how relieved I was that he was also getting help. "I was afraid we'd lost you," I said. Then, I told him how much I loved him. "Love, Sister."

He replied with a favorable rehab review: "When you meet someone in rehab, your very first conversation is 'I stabbed a guy on meth' or whatever. Just very open here." He seemed content overall. He liked the people, the food, and even the sobriety. He sounded enthusiastic about the journey. I was confident that he was finally in good hands and headed in the right direction.

We talked on the phone later that week during a rare sleeping-baby moment. And I mean *rare*. Harris and I seldom talked on the phone, but he called often in rehab. He seemed eager to reconnect with the family, to rebuild. My mom and I were both struck by the literal tone and pitch of his voice. It was different. He sounded awake for the first time since all this madness began. We talked for a long time that night. He admitted to taking twenty Oxys the night before he went to rehab and not even feeling high. "Okay, I have a problem," he finally admitted to himself. "Rehab is the only option or I will die." He vomited in the cab on the way to the facility.

Harris asked a ton of questions about how I was feeling and coping and really listened to my answers. He was unbelievably present. It was sort of unfamiliar. When I described how terrified I was about all of Iris's upcoming medical tests, he coached me to stop future-tripping. "Today is all we have for sure," he said. *Maybe I should go to rehab*, I thought.

I was sitting on the sofa in my parents' living room as we talked, staring at the framed needlepoint picture that hangs above the doorway in their kitchen. It says: "God grant me the serenity to accept the things I cannot change, the courage to change the things I can, and the wisdom to know the difference." My mom made it long ago, before we were born. It hung on the wall in our breakfast room when we were growing up, directly across from where I always sat at the table, right above Harris's head. It was always there in my line of vision, but I never really *saw* it until now. On the other end of the line, my brother told me they say this prayer at the end of every meeting.

I was bludgeoned by a notion that hadn't struck me until now: we were the same. We both had to surrender to our shitty circumstances and "accept the things we cannot change." We both agreed that we had to at least *try* to take it one day at a time.

Neither of us had any idea how to do that.

# 12

## Four Months, Two Weeks, Six Days

Getting rid of your things is difficult. Most of the furniture went to the Upright Citizen's Brigade green room in LA. They also took the piano that came with the house. The kitchen stuff went to Goodwill. Your massive DVD collection went to our friend Johnny. The drums went to our friend Danny. Various friends took the T-shirts. The Phish posters went to Matt Marcus, who drove the BMW back to Houston, where Mike and I traded it in for a Subaru. We sold the two ridiculously large televisions and stereo equipment to friends of friends. Iris got your vintage Happy Meal toys, Teenage Mutant Ninja Turtles, Simpsons characters, and other plastic action figures from childhood. She also swiped a large rock from outside your house. She collects them.

The actual house is the last big thing to go, and it happened today. As we slept, the funds were transferred into our account via direct deposit—just like that. All your toil, sleepless nights, and parasitic stress compressed into a series of numbers on a screen, a screen that didn't even belong to you. One time when I was guilt-tripping you about getting sober, you jokingly said, "Hey, if I die, you'll be rich!" I told you it wasn't funny. While we're certainly not rich, we can now afford to look at houses in central Houston that are zoned to our first-choice elementary school. Ambivalent doesn't even begin to describe how I feel.

My father-in-law, a real estate agent who lives in Long Beach, took care of the sale. He made the repairs, staged it nicely, and put it on the market. He handled the closing, while we remained back home in Houston. It's a nice house in a desirable neighborhood, so it didn't take long to sell. And now it's gone. New residents—retirees—who likely don't have a print hanging in their foyer of naked Kristen Stewarts floating around the cosmos on raw steaks.

I wonder if they know what happened in this house.

I remember when you started house hunting in 2011. We spent hours chatting about the process online. You'd send me listings, I'd scrutinize them, and we'd compare notes.

> **Me:** WOW
> that is gorgeous
> i love that house
> **Harris:** the problem with that one is no backyard really.
> **Me:** less work for you
> **Harris:** it was owned by a gay dude so it is beautiful
> **Me:** there are still outdoor spaces
> **Harris:** and this next one i truly love and there is this huge back-
> yard where i could do whatever i want. put a pool in, whatever.
> but its up a TON of stairs
> but look at that insane view
> **Me:** that is a shit ton of stairs
> but very pretty
> you have traditional taste
> like mom

**Harris:** like in terms of what

what taste do u have?

i mean ignore the furniture

**Me:** contemporary gay

**Harris:** i love contemporary gay!

i love that first house

just wish it had more space

**Me:** the first house is right up my alley

i dont love the brown marble and marble in general on the

2nd one

but again, that's a taste issue

**Harris:** i dont either

**Me:** like, that kitchen omg

**Harris:** that kitchen is like the kitchen we grew up in

**Me:** i know exactly!

i was thinking that

mom would love it

The one you eventually settled on sat at the foot of Griffith Park in Los Feliz. It resembled the brick, 1950s ranch-style home we grew up in, one block away from our neighborhood middle school. Three bedrooms, two and a half baths, one story—a modest abode, relatively speaking. Orangish-reddish brick. White trim. Traditional. It could have blended into any residential neighborhood in Houston. You were specifically looking for a house like this, something familiar and cozy in a place that didn't always feel like those things.

The backyard was of paramount importance to you. It was your favorite spot. I can see you sitting out there on the patio at the round, metal table with the overflowing ashtrays, one knee folded up in the chair, smoking cigarette after cigarette, sending swarms of texts, recording beloved Vines.

We had a table like that in our backyard growing up. In high school, my friends and I would sit out there after Mom and Dad went to bed and chain-smoke our teenage lives away. Ironically, you weren't much of a smoker back then, which is why your excessive smoking as an adult has always baffled me.

I recently found this picture you drew of us back in high school, depicting our morning car rides. We overlapped one year: you were a freshman; I was senior. In the drawing, Ani DiFranco (my permanent high-school music choice) is blaring through the speakers. The *Tae Bo people* are these old people who did Tai Chi on the lawn of this Hasidic synagogue that we drove by every morning. I'm smoking. You hated it when I smoked in the car and made *the biggest fucking deal* about how it was killing you and aggravating your allergies.

In February, when we were in LA packing up your house, Mom and I were surprised to find canvases, art supplies, an easel, and several finished paintings in your guest room. One of them sits in my closet now. I look at it daily. The background is a deep, dark blue with splotches of black. Several stars made of tin foil speckle the sky. A veiny pink and red heart with yellow-gold wings flies up to the heavens. White dots border the top and the sides of the flying heart, while red dots drip off the bottom. The lower portion of the painting depicts the ground, the earth. Black, barren trees sit on a black landscape. There is a large, hollow skull perched in the bottom left corner, also lined with dots. The earth is bleak; the sky is where the heart takes flight.

I had no idea you were painting.

Selling your house depletes me. Just one more piece of evidence that this is really happening.

In addition to selling *your* house, we've also listed ours in Houston. I can't get out of here fast enough. It's too small, there's bad juju, and I'm still scarred from the mold fiasco that left us displaced last year for six weeks and cost $8,000 in repairs, none of which was covered by insurance nor recouped from the previous owners.

Mom's voice echoes inside my head: "Life isn't fair, Stephanie."

Originally, Mike tried to sell the house for $150 and a two-hundred-word essay. The idea was that we'd get enough money from entry fees to cover the cost of the home, someone would get a charming house in a cool neighborhood for $150, and he'd get some decent publicity as a real estate agent. This was necessary because—*head's up*—when your wife is consumed with crippling grief and either weeping, sleeping, or generally catatonic, you wind up with lots of extra shit on your plate. He had basically put his career on the back burner since February, and it was time to initiate some sort of resurrection.

Man, if I thought our story was sad…holy fuck. Want to feel better about your life? List your house for $150 and have people submit essays about why they need it. I had to stop reading them after a while. Also, the media attention was overwhelming and made my anxiety flare up. People were driving by at all hours of the day and night to check out the house, which isn't exactly comforting with a baby inside. A couple of people even knocked on the front door and asked to take a look around. The story ran in every local publication, moved on to national headlines in the *New York Times, NPR,* and *Businessweek,* and eventually made its way over to Britain and parts of Europe. Another runaway train of a situation.

Even though we received nearly three thousand essays, only half of the applicants paid, so there wasn't enough to cover the cost of the house, and we could've extended the deadline, but I got paranoid that we were breaking some law by running what could be considered an illegal raffle and didn't want my husband to go to jail on top of all the other shit that was going on. So, at the end of June, we called it quits, and Mike listed the house the traditional way. Fortunately, it only took a day for someone to make an offer.

During the inspection, which takes place the day after we sell your house, the potential buyer is walking around the attic, and his foot falls through the ceiling. *Literally.* And the rotting drywall, on the way down, scratches that print that used to hang in your dining room of all the pop icons—one of the things that most reminds me of you. I spent so much time in your house over the years staring at it, trying to figure out the identity of each character. And now it's permanently banged up by a piece of old, rotten drywall that fell from the ceiling in this cursed, piece of shit house. Just heap it on top of the giant pile that my soul is buried under.

Sometimes I think about you being buried in the ground. I think about what color your skin is, the texture. I see a sort of shade of gray. I wonder how your arms are positioned and what your face is doing. You had such a great face.

# 13

### Five Months

Every morning when I open my eyes, I think of Iris and then I think of you. You two are so fused together in my mind. The year she was born, I worried so much about both of you. This comes with the territory of motherhood. I am her mother now, but I mothered you first. After I stopped stealing your toys and hating you for stealing Mom, I cared for you. You were my little brother. *Were* or *are*? Past or present? It still says you're my brother on Facebook. But you're no longer *here* to be my brother. So, am I still a sister? Is *sister* a verb or a noun? Is it something you have to actively do to be one, or do you keep the title once the other half is gone?

When I was your sister, actively, I protected you. I paid for you. I felt responsible for you. I kept all your darkest secrets. I loved you ferociously. When we went to clean out your house, I went on a shredding spree, convinced random people would rummage through the trash. Looking back, I don't even remember what I shredded. Entries in your journal from rehab. Some stuff in a shoebox in the closet of your guest room. Love letters, maybe? I didn't even read them. I just felt such an instinct to protect you even after you were gone.

I wonder if I will ever open my eyes and not think of you within those first few moments. I don't see how it's possible. I wonder if you are the first thing on Mom's mind when she opens her eyes. Surely. We mothers think of our children first—*always*.

When we look at photos together now, Iris says everyone's name but yours, a constant reminder that she will never know you. She says *Momo, Bapa, Mommy, Daddy, Iris*…then she gets to your face and goes silent. In one black-and-white family photo from 2010 that I carry in my wallet, she thinks you look like Mike and calls you "Daddy" (gross). Whenever I show her baby pictures of you, she shouts "Iris!" She thinks it's her. It could be. There's a strong likeness.

God, I wish you could be here to watch her grow. She's so cool. And smart. And funny. She often prances around the house in a pink leotard with butterfly wings sewed onto the back and forces Mike and I to partake in endless rounds of "Ring Around the Rosie," drowning in laughter every time we all fall down. She knows all her animal sounds and shapes and colors. She laser-focuses on any movie from start to finish—crying at the sad parts, laughing at the funny parts. Her sense of empathy is astounding. She makes an angry face and a happy face and a surprised face and a worried face on command. She's wildly sensitive—a tiny tornado of feelings. She's a force. And loving. So loving.

I worry about how all of this will affect her—babies absorb it all—but every day provides further proof that neither her hearing loss nor the overwhelming grief that has swallowed her mother whole has had any impact on her development. She's a happy and well-adjusted child who blows kisses with every hello and goodbye; a wave will not suffice. Every speech evaluation thus far has put her well ahead of the curve. She goes to a regular preschool with hearing kids and needs no special accommodations. Because we were so aggressive with early intervention, narrating every moment of her life that first year, attending speech therapy every two weeks, which turned into monthly, which turned into quarterly, which turned into bi-annually, she has morphed into a baby talk machine. Nothing is slowing her down.

This morning, she pulls out a stuffed frog that I took from your house—one of many stuffed animals lying around. You really were like Tom Hanks's character in *Big*. (You loved that movie, justifiably so.) The tag still attached reads *Fiesta*. It's the only plush toy in the bin with the tag still attached, but I want to preserve its authenticity. I have such a reflexive urge to text you and ask you where you got this shitty little frog with the Fiesta tag. Instead, I look into the frog's beady little eyes and futilely ask him for an answer.

Then, Iris brings over this little yellow book called *Hand Hand Fingers Thumb* about millions of drumming monkeys. (You were a drummer.) At that moment, there's a huge crash of thunder, and the power goes out for a split second. I walk into the bedroom to check in with Mike, and the digital clock reads 4:20. Your birthday.

1. The frog.
2. The drumming monkeys.
3. The thunder.
4. The blackout.
5. Your birthday.

All in a matter of moments.
Is it you? Or is this what the grieving do?
Do we need to find meaning in the mundane?

Do we need to make connections where coincidences used to occur? Is this what we have to do to keep going?

Iris has her six-month follow-up hearing test in the morning. Needless to say, I feel like I might die of an anxiety attack. It's in these moments that I would text you and freak out and you would reassure me that it would be fine, and you would say it in such a way that made me feel ridiculous for even stressing about it in the first place. Only you could do that.

So, I do what any grief-stricken, crazy person would do and talk to you out loud like you're a spirit or a ghost or something. I ask you to watch over Iris tomorrow and protect her. I've literally never talked out loud to something or someone who isn't there. (I mean, I did it at the cemetery, but you were kind of there, beneath me.) Mid-conversation, I ask: "Are you listening to me, Harris?" And I look out the window at the sky, and in my mind, I think, *If you are listening to me, make a bird fly across the sky right now*, and right then, three birds fly across the sky. My heart sinks in a good way. I smile. My eyes water.

I tell Mike about my "conversation" with you later that night before we go to bed.

"That's a lot of pressure to put on a dead person," he says.

Now, every morning, I open the blinds over the kitchen sink and say hi and wait for a bird to fly by. This is probably what crazy people do. And then there are these tiny, white feathers all over my front and back yard. My neighbors on either side have none. Maybe my yard has always been littered with tiny white feathers and I just never noticed, but now they're all I see. Mom told me a white feather is a sign from your loved one up in heaven. I felt sorry for her at the time that she had to cling to such a delusional notion for comfort. But now I see white feathers *everywhere*. The other day, one floated right in front of my face in the car. Like, while I was driving. And it's a sign that you're still here. You're in everything, but your everythingness no longer makes me hit the ground. Rather, it brings an unfamiliar sense of peace and comfort.

I mean, is this what God feels like? I certainly don't want to compare my dead brother to God, but the feeling that some sort of invisible energy or spirit is out there and accessible is wholly unfamiliar. People always say things like: "Oh, I don't believe in God, but I'm spiritual." I'm not even "spiritual." Neither were you. This is why you always got hung up on the Twelve Steps. The higher power was always too elusive.

I've always turned to my loved ones, my therapist, my pattern of feeling my feelings deeply, making ahas, and moving on in a positive direction having learned something deeper about myself and the world. I haven't ever turned to something invisible. I've never felt like something up above had my back. But now I sort of feel like someone in the universe is looking out for me. For the first time in my life, I have faith in something larger than myself: I have faith in the spirit of Harris.

This sounds like something a defense attorney could use in a court of law as proof that a person has come undone. But I know that, for now, in order to get out of bed every morning, in order to put one foot in front of the other, I need to believe it's true.

By the way, the hearing test went fine. There's been no change, and her hearing loss is still stable. For now.

Thank you, Harris.

# 14

—

## Before

### July 2014

A few months after Harris got out of the fancy rehab in Malibu, my parents, the baby, Mike, and I met him in Park City, Utah, for our annual summer vacation. I was hoping for an escape from The Land of Hearing-Loss Hysteria, and much of the trip served its purpose. By day, we took the baby on her first train ride; by night, we played rounds and rounds of Mexican Train as a family at the dining room table in the hotel suite we all shared. One afternoon, Mike's mom and her boyfriend traveled in from Scottsdale, and we met them for high tea at this fancy hotel in downtown Salt Lake City. Another day, we went to a big, outdoor farmers' market where we got Iris these superfly, handmade, yellow moccasins that she wore on her feet until they all but unraveled. Uncle Harris made sure she tasted her first Dippin' Dots.

I was eager to bond with my brother on this trip—my *real* brother, not my junkie brother. My real brother was the coolest, funniest, kindest guy in the whole wide world.

Unfortunately, it was clear very quickly that this was not the Harris who showed up. This one had lost the pep in his sober step.

He was mostly in a bad mood, sleeping late, smoking excessively. The bags under his eyes and the oil in his hair were highlighted by the iPhone screen that he held in front of his face for most of the trip. One day, in the parking garage of our hotel, he went off on an angry rant about how his boss at *Parks* wouldn't promote him after he'd been there for six seasons. This was the same boss who had been extremely supportive of Harris taking as much time as he needed to go to rehab in the first place. Mike and I were caught off-guard. It was crystal clear to us why his boss has made this decision, but Harris wasn't exactly working from a place of self-awareness.

Another day, driving into town on the bus, he was scrolling through the AA Meetings Finder app and made a comment about how stupid it was that he couldn't just drink one beer. "I never had a problem with alcohol in the first place—I don't even like alcohol. Why can't I just have a fucking beer like a normal person?" He opened the app several times but didn't go to a single meeting the whole week. When I questioned him, he swore he was sober. I was certain he wasn't. I didn't know what to do, so I chose to feign ignorance.

After the vacation, we went back to our lives. Weeks passed. School resumed. It was hard to be present for several reasons. Every day, I found new cracks in the walls of our house. My brother was likely back on drugs. I missed my infant child every minute of every day now that I was back at work. I had to take an impractical break every few hours to pump milk from my engorged breasts in a glorified closet. I tried to do it all. It was hard, but I tried. I cried every day.

And then everything got much, *much* worse.

It was 4:15 p.m. on a weekday. I remember how the sun was shining through the blinds, painting stripes of light on the kitchen table. I remember picking up the phone from the kitchen table and reading this text from my brother:

> Hey I'm gonna call mom and dad later but heads up I'm checking back into rehab tomorrow in Oregon. I started shooting heroin.
>
> My sponsor is with me now babysitting. My boss knows.
>
> I'm fine and alive.

My heart stopped.

*He was shooting heroin?*

My mom happened to be at my house that afternoon. When she saw my face fall, she read the text over my shoulder and immediately erupted into wild, guttural sobs. She hit the floor and screamed, *"No, no, no, no, NO!"* In hysterics, she called my dad and screamed the news into the phone: "He's gonna die, Ellison! He's going to kill himself!" My dad, likely in shock, paused for an inordinately long time. Being a person who functions in a black-and-white world, it's like he short-circuited and wasn't able to process, handle, or accept this news. Harris had already gone to rehab. He had already gotten sober. The problem was solved six months ago. Why were we back at the problem? Why had the problem gotten worse? From his vantage point, Harris sabotaged his sobriety. This was Harris's fault. He told my mom he no longer wanted a relationship with Harris. He was done. Having a son who was a heroin addict just wasn't something he was willing to accept.

In hindsight, our reaction was strange. We all knew he was a drug addict—this wasn't news—but for some reason, being addicted to something for which you can be medically prescribed and take with a glass of water felt more dignified than cooking dirty, brown powder in a spoon, pouring it into a needle, and injecting it into your arm or in between your toes. Now that he was shooting heroin, it finally hit us like a bold, headline in block text on the front page of a newspaper: **HARRIS IS A DRUG ADDICT. HE REALLY IS A DRUG ADDICT. THIS IS REALLY HAPPENING. WAKE UP.**

Harris and I talked on the phone that night. I cried. I don't think it landed on him. I don't think he even heard it. He was probably high.

"How did this happen?"

"It happened because I was curious, and it's cheap, and pills are hard to come by."

"How did you even know how to do that?"

"That part isn't hard. There's YouTube."

"So, you were alone or with friends?"

"Alone."

So, he'd been sitting alone, in his house, watching YouTube videos, and sticking needles in his arms. What the fuck, Harris? What the fuck?

At 1:47 a.m., he sent me a text.

I feel really bad about mom.

I didn't respond until 5:30 a.m. when I woke up to feed the baby.

Yeah I can't really sugar coat it. She's pretty destroyed. Never seen her like that. And dad is really angry. We have all been dealing with so much pain and anxiety and uncertainty and grief with Iris. Every day is a struggle. I can't remember the last time I went a day without crying. And now this. It's a lot. It's too much. I am not trying to make you feel worse or guilty. I'm just being honest because I am too exhausted to be anything else.

One of my all-time favorite photos of you and Iris was taken last summer on that family vacation to Utah. It now serves as my screen saver. In it, Iris is just six months old. It's a crisp, sunny day. The mountains are in the background. She's sitting in her stroller, bare-foot, wearing a fuchsia, chevron-patterned sun hat. In one hand, she holds my scarf; in the other, she covers your mouth with her tiny hand. You are kneeling down, leaning over the side of the stroller. Your face and neck are covered by scruff. You've got that scar over your eyebrow from the time when you were two years old and fell face first on the back steps of our house in Oklahoma. They were red brick. You got a gigantic, gushing gash over your left eyebrow that left a permanent scar. As you were bleeding out in your car seat, I was searching my room for my pink jelly shoes. I'd tracked down one but not the other. Dad came in shouting at me to get in the car. I tried to explain my predicament, but he scooped me up before I could track down the other one, and I went to the hospital wearing one shoe.

On your head rests your blue, *Just Be Cool* baseball cap. You're wearing dark Ray-Bans, but I can see you staring into her eyes from the side of the glasses. And she's staring right back into yours. You are both totally relaxed and at peace. Neither of you is aware that someone is permanently capturing this moment that will eventually sit on a screensaver. This makes it the best kind of photo.

Sometimes I clear all the windows from my desktop and trace the outline of your nose with my fingertip. You had the perfect profile—such a perfectly shaped nose. It took you a while to grow into it, but when you did, the ladies lined up. You used to say every girl had, at minimum, a 20 percent crush on you.

## 15

—

## Five Months, One Week, Two Days

At the end of July, a popular media outlet is gracious enough to post the results of your autopsy all over the internet before our family is even notified that the report has been completed. And now hundreds of people are flocking to the Facebook comment thread to post things like "He deserved it," "What an idiot," "He's just a junkie," and my personal favorite: "Anyone who sticks a needle in their arm deserves to die and elicits no sympathy from me."

My heart beat ramps up, my face gets hot, and I want to respond, "You are correct, person on Facebook: there is truly no sympathy from you. No bad things will *ever* happen to you. You will never experience pain and suffering. Your life will always be as it is: idyllic. Continue to sprawl out on your puffy, white cloud eating cotton candy and grapes from the vine as you look down on the rest of us."

But I don't. Because what's the point? It won't change anyone's mind. No one's come here to try to understand the complex nuances of addiction. Rather, I'll post something heartfelt and sincere that I work really hard to craft, only to get bombarded with notification upon notification of even shittier, even *more* insensitive comments.

It's the fucking Wild West. There's no place for empathy and understanding; it's all jabs and tirades and vitriol with no consideration of who's on the receiving end, being told her only brother was a junkie who deserved to die.

I mean, who *are* these people? Did they not go to elementary school? Did they never learn the Golden Rule? This variety of internet hatred lodges itself so deeply under my skin, like a parasite. How can fellow human beings hate-post so casually about things that seem unfuckwithable? Like you. And Iris.

Another thing you've missed is my newfound political activism. These last couple of months, in an attempt to find somewhere to displace my rage, I've been fighting for insurance coverage of children's hearing aids in the state of Texas. Even though every single medical professional we've encountered since Day One of Iris's diagnosis has continued to stress the importance of technology and early intervention for speech, language, and brain development in kids who are hard of hearing, hearing aids are considered "cosmetic" and cost up to $6,000 out of pocket every three to five years. You know this because I complained about it relentlessly when you were alive. It's maddening.

Earlier this month, we lost the legislative battle for a number of reasons—chief among them: life isn't fair—but I recently wrote a scathing op-ed for the *Houston Chronicle* about the inefficacy of the Texas Legislature. In it, I mentioned that hearing loss is often genetic, so many families have multiple children in need of the technology, which is a heavy financial burden. In the comments section, a true internet angel posted: "If it is genetic *don't have children*!!!" Then, another commenter echoed her sentiments: "That is what I was thinking, adopt."

*Can you motherfucking believe that shit?*

I mean, clearly they're right! I never should have had my healthy, beautiful, sweet, hilarious, smart, loving, perfect two-year-old because she has hearing loss. Every other person in the history of the world is genetically perfect. What a bummer for us!

It's just so carelessly brazen and devoid of empathy. Is it not in the realm of possibility that an internet troll could love someone who is born deaf or who chooses to stick needles in their arms? Isn't that what empathy is? Putting myself in someone else's shoes with the knowledge and awareness that I, too, am human and, therefore, susceptible to this tragedy or any number of tragedies along the way?

Maybe people are just shitty. Or maybe it's the internet's fault. Or maybe people are just shitty and it's the internet's fault.

Regardless, I wish you were still here and not the subject of an autopsy report that was recently posted online for internet trolls to feed on.

I email the detective who called me that beautiful day in February to tell me you were dead. I ask where I can obtain a copy of the report and why we weren't notified. She responds quickly, informing me that it's public record now and I can go online to their website and order one for twenty-six dollars, like I'm renewing a driver's license. I think about emailing the author of the recently published article and asking if I can just borrow his.

I buy the report even though it won't be groundbreaking news. You died of a heroin overdose: case closed. But reading all of the online commentary about you brings it all back to that first week after you died. Having to see the tragedy unfold in public the first time was hard enough. I don't want to do this again.

When the big, yellow envelope arrives in the mail one week later, I set it on the counter where it sits all night underneath an Anthropologie catalogue while Mike and I drink a bottle of wine with a friend. Just glancing over at it makes my heart bang around in my chest and my hands shake, and I want to throw it away or send it back or pretend it never came. But I can't. When our friend leaves and Mike steps outside to walk the dog, I finally have a quiet moment to sit alone on the bed and spill my tears onto a fourteen-page report over your dead body.

> *From the anatomic findings and pertinent history I ascribe the death to:*
> **Acute heroin intoxication.**
>
> *Anatomical Summary:*
> Pulmonary edema.
> Focal 5–10% atherosclerosis of the LAD coronary artery. Other coronaries are clean.

There are many medical terms I have to Google.

There are several diagrams, one outlining the rigor mortis scale of various body parts during the detective's investigation. The scale is from 0 (Absent/Negative) to 4 (Extreme Degree). You were at a 2 across the board.

There are checklists and columns of body parts and organs that were "dissected," their respective weights (in grams), and whether or not they were within normal limits.

Right lung: 655 grams

Left lung: 675 grams

Spleen: 340 grams

Liver: 1750 grams

Right kidney: 130 grams

Left kidney: 130 grams

Heart: 325 grams

Brain: 1350 grams

There is a toxicology report: Opiates. All opiates.

There is a case report with stuff like "911 was dialed and LAFD pronounced death on scene at 1200 hours without medical intervention" and "No foul play was suspected."

There is a detailed report of how your body was positioned on the floor and where abrasions, punctures, and bruises were found, along with a description of the "scene" (they call it a *scene*) that reads like stage directions from a play. There's something almost poetic about it.

The scene was the living room in a northwestern area of a single-story residence. The decedent was observed supine on a rug adjacent to an L-shaped sofa. A white paramedic sheet was partially covering the decedent. A lighter was grasped in his right hand. A backpack on the floor of the living room contained a 'Narcotics Anonymous' book.

There was no evidence of end of life activity or suicidal notes.

He had short brown hair, brown eyes, beard,

mustache, and natural teeth. He was clad in a white t-shirt, brown pants, blue socks, and a brown belt. Blood was emitting from the nose and mouth. His jaw was clenched with the tip of his tongue between his teeth.

His jaw was clenched with the tip of his tongue between his teeth.

On 2/19/2015 at 1515 hours I notified the decedent's sister, Stephanie Wittels, of the death via telephone.

# 16

—

## Six Months, One Week

Despite how shitty I feel, life events keep happening as life events do. Not long after the autopsy report is released to the public, we move out of our tiny, cursed, ceiling-falling, foundation-shifting, mold-inducing, rodent-infested house. The new house is significantly bigger and newer and generally nicer. I'm not afraid to walk into the kitchen at night in bare feet. I'm hoping we'll have a fresh start. The attic has been converted into a third-floor playroom that we will soon paint from floor to ceiling with giant jungle animals. There's a place to put all of Iris's things. There's a place to put all our things. We finally clean out the storage unit, and now there's a place to put all *your* things.

The gorgeous, mid-century modern chest of drawers that sat in your entryway now lives in my dining room. The bottom-right drawer is stuffed with all of Iris's artwork from her little Montessori preschool. I keep thinking I need to do something more with it, but I'm not crafty, so there it sits. Iris pulls all of it out to show Momo and Bapa whenever they come over. She's proud of her work. She calls it her "work." Montessori lingo is adorable.

Your two cushiony, vintage chairs that spin around and swallow you up sit in our living room on top of the enormous shaggy rug where you lay dead six months ago. I thought about throwing it out, but I just couldn't part with it. It's not even particularly nice. I actually think you got it at IKEA. But it was yours. And I like to be surrounded by you. Sometimes I lay on it, too.

Upstairs in our bedroom are two more mid-century modern chests of drawers and the epic, wood-grained lamps that hugged either side of your bed. The TV in our bedroom sits on the same piece of furniture you used.

We are surrounded by you.

Most of the art that hung in your house now hangs in ours:

1. The giant painting of the boat sailing through choppy ocean waters that hung above your fireplace now hangs in our foyer.
2. The colorful ink drawing with all the little triangles and swirls and dotted lines and geometric shapes hangs across from the painting of the boat.
3. The large Johnny Carson painting is above our kitchen table. I imagine that you got it from a yard sale. It has a very yard-sale vibe. Johnny Carson obviously looks nothing like Mike, who has dark brown hair and a full beard, but Iris always looks at the painting while we eat and says, "Daddy!"
4. Above the stove hangs the hand-carved, wooden State of Indiana with the star over Pawnee. The engraving on the back says *For 125 Episodes of Love, Chuckles & Breakfast. We Love You Forever. The Cast.*
5. The scratched print of the pop icons is in the dining room.
6. The collage of butterfly wings is on the landing of the stairs.

7. The what-we-believe-to-be-David-Choe piece is in the hallway right outside of Iris's room.

8. I framed those neon-colored prints that were collecting dust in your desk drawer and hung them in her room. I have no idea why you had them or what they were doing in your desk drawer, but they say *Hello World*, *Excited*, and *High Hopes*. Perfect for a little being with her long life stretched out before her.

9. The Japanese landscape made of stones and rocks of varying shapes, sizes, and colors that used to hang in Grandma's house, the one you laid claim to when we were cleaning out her house after *she* died, now lives in our living room. This is what happens in families. You just pass shit down and around when people die. I remember being pissed at the time that you got that piece. And now I have it. It all feeds into the same stream.

The move, like any move, involves taking stock of what needs to go in a box and what doesn't. File cabinets are land mines for the grieving. Folders full of keepsakes and birthday cards and happy times captured in actual photos that you can hold in your hands. These feel so much sadder than the digital ones.

In a folder titled *Miscellaneous*, I find a letter you wrote me from Blue Star Camp in the summer of 1997. You were thirteen and not into capitalization. A regular e. e. cummings.

> *dear steph,*
> *they have computers so i decided to type u a letter. camp's*
> *cool. i hooked up with monica again but i haven't done*

*anything u wouldn't do. 311 is o.k. how's big ben? i miss a good ass whoopin every now and then. how's houston? we went to carowinds. it's like a white trash astroworld. it was really fun. i met a lot of new friends. one is matt. he lives in l.a. i want to go to his bar mitzvah with benji really bad but i doubt mom and dad will let me. are mom and dad getting it on every night because i'm at camp? i went bowling and pissed some carolina hicks off. i have to go to basketball now but i'll see you in a week n a half. i love u.*

*love, harris*

At some point along the way, you got into the habit of starting notes or emails with *Dear Sister*, and signing them *Love, Brother*. I'll never see that again. No one else in the world can ever sign a letter to me that way.

When you lose a sibling, you lose a huge piece of your identity.

Your history.

Your context.

It's the loneliest feeling.

# 17

—

## Before

### August 2014

The day after Harris informed me via text message that he had started shooting heroin, he went back to rehab for another thirty-day stint. The first rehab was in Malibu; the second one was somewhere in the middle of Oregon. His AA sponsor got him in.

From what I could glean over the phone and via email, he seemed to be doing the work, but I got the impression that the program *felt* like work this time around. His voice was less animated and enthusiastic than it was at rehab number one. The novelty of rehab had worn off. Part of the issue was that he'd gone from the Ritz Carlton to the Holiday Inn. It was no longer a spa retreat. No gourmet chefs or ocean views included. The last rehab had the glisten of newness, hope, and promise. This time around, he checked in already feeling like a failure. At the last rehab, he was a shining star. His therapist reported to my mom over the phone one day that only one (maybe two) out of the twenty that were currently enrolled would remain sober once they got out. Those were the odds. Pretty bleak. But she anticipated that Harris would be one of the lucky few. He was just so committed to doing the work. She could see that he really wanted it, that he was genuinely invested in staying sober.

At the end of the thirty days, my mom flew out to Oregon for Family Weekend, alone. My dad didn't want to go. Again. He's not a feeler by nature, so when things like this come up, he shuts down. He did the same thing to me when I was fifteen and made a significant error in judgment. He ignored me for weeks and neglected to see that I hated myself enough for the both of us. He didn't have to take any of the blame—I had it all covered. At the time, I wanted so badly to grab him and hug him and tell him I was sorry and that I loved him. But I didn't, and neither did he. Time passed, it was swept under the rug, and we moved forward.

But here he was, nearly twenty years later, doing it again. What I understand now that I didn't understand then is that he wasn't ignoring me to punish me. He was ignoring me because he was punishing himself. When his children failed, it wasn't their fault. It was *his*.

He needed to call his son and get on a plane and look him in the eye and love him through this because that's what love is and that's what the boy needed. But stoic he remained. My mom couldn't get through to him. I couldn't get through to him. I wanted to shake him out of his catatonia, but he seemed so fragile underneath all the effort to hold it together that I was afraid I might break him, so I didn't.

My mom was nervous about the weekend. Once she got there, she had to spend the bulk of her days in meetings with strangers about addiction being a family disease. She was only able to see my brother for about an hour each day. She was lonely and sad. She wanted to do whatever it took to help her son but felt so out of place there. I had the urge to rescue her but had a baby who relied on breast milk, so I couldn't.

Harris's plan was to go to rehab for thirty days, then come back to Houston for a while, see the baby, and regroup. But toward the end of treatment, he changed his mind. When we talked about it over the phone, he blamed it on my dad. He said he still felt a lot of shame and didn't want to put his recovery in jeopardy, so he would just go back to LA. Where he started shooting heroin in the first place.

After he served his time, he checked out and spent the night in the hotel with my mom. She reported back to me that it felt different than the last time he got out. His vibe wasn't particularly open or communicative or refreshed. He was impatient and on edge. He seemed as closed off as he was when he arrived a month ago. Sobriety had lost its luster.

Once she got back to Houston, my mom started attending regular Al-Anon meetings. She'd always been willing to do anything for her children, whether it be chaperoning a field trip or going to an Al-Anon meeting. She was always a good and loving mother. Now she was a good and loving mother who woke up every day worried that it would be her son's last.

# 18

—

## Seven Months

You always said you'd take Mom to the Emmys someday, and here we are—she and I—standing in a large dressing room with cheap maroon carpet, staring into a mirror, draped in gowns strewn with beads and sparkles and rhinestones. I've never worn a gown like this. It's so heavy. I imagine I'll have to wear shapewear. I hate shapewear. I hate you for putting me in this position.

This is not how any of us imagined this would play out. In the future fantasy scenario, Mom is your date. You'd strut the red carpet together, hobnobbing with celebs as she clung proudly to your arm. You'd thank her in your acceptance speech as the camera panned over to her, dabbing her wet eyes with a tissue. Dad and I would proudly watch it all unfold on TV back in Houston. I would be wearing an elastic waistband, *not* a gown.

In three weeks, Mom and I are going to the Emmys without you. *Parks and Recreation* is nominated for Best Comedy Series, and you will be honored in the In Memoriam segment. An invite showed up in Mom's in-box late August. She forwarded it to me with the overly exuberant message: "Please go with me!!!!!!!!!!" She still composes emails in Comic Sans, which just adds to my frustration about the entire ordeal.

I was at work. I audibly grumbled. There was no way to get out of this.

The timing is terrible. My students just got back from summer break. We just moved into our new house a week ago. There are so many tchotchkes to shelve. I don't want to leave my family for three days. I don't want to take a day off work. I don't want to fly to Los Angeles ever again. I don't want to go to an awards ceremony in honor of my dead brother. Once again, why can't Dad go? Why can't he play the part of supportive husband? It's landed on my desk since you died, and I never applied for the job.

I explain all my reasons to Mom but end the email saying I'll go if it's really important to her. As you know, she brings that out in people.

"It's really important to me!!!!!!!" Again with the fucking exclamation marks. It's too much punctuation with which to argue.

We book the tickets and buy the gowns. I go with one that has zero beading but plenty of flare. The top is silver and shiny like a fashionable suit of armor. The bottom part is a floor-length chiffon skirt with big silver and white horizontal stripes. Describing it makes it sound hideous, but it was quite beautiful. The only thing I've ever worn that comes close to this level of formality was my wedding dress. Mom goes for a white Monique Lhuillier beaded gown. I assume she'll have to pay extra for luggage. It's so fucking heavy.

The day before we leave for LA, Mom gets an email from Universal inviting us to an NBC pre-party on Saturday night. As much as I don't want to go the Emmys, I *really* don't want to go to this. None of this feels like a party. Plus, you hated these sorts of things. Mom, of course, feels otherwise and wants to see "famous people."

106

She also feels it necessary to remind me *several times* to pack my dress and my shoes like I'm a fucking five-year-old. My frustration with her is reaching levels only experienced as an angsty teen living under the same roof. She is genuinely excited about the weekend. It is off-putting. She seems to have lost sight of the fact that we are going because you died.

We're walking to the gate at the airport on Saturday afternoon when she says, "I am just so excited that you finally get a little vacation. You never get to relax!" The invisible tape I've put over my mouth out of respect for our grieving mother finally rips off. "Mom, we're going to the Emmys because Harris died. Nothing about this is relaxing. I don't even want to go."

She's stunned. Silence steals the space between us. We wait for the plane in silence, board the plane in silence, take off in silence. I can tell that she is genuinely hurt and throwing a silent temper tantrum of epic proportions. I recognize in this moment what my therapist was describing in our last session: my mother has conflated our emotional experiences. If she wants to go to the Emmys, I want to go to the Emmys. If she feels excited, I feel excited. This must be some residue of emotional grief.

Soon, the flight attendant rolls by to take drink orders. I order a white wine, crack open the top, pour it in the plastic cup, take a big sip, and turn to Mom.

"So, are you gonna ignore me the rest of the trip?"

"I just feel very guilty now," she says in her delicate Southern drawl. "I forced you to come with me, and you don't want to be here."

"You didn't force me. It's just so hard to leave the baby. It's a lot for Mike—"

"I know. I feel *terrible*."

And now I feel terrible.

"Mom, it's fine. I wanted to be here for you. Am I not allowed to be honest about how I feel?"

It goes back and forth like this for several minutes, she playing the *I feel so guilty* card, and I, the *I want to be here/It's fine* one.

Finally, I finish the wine and beg: "Can we just move past this and try to have a good time this weekend? I don't have the energy to argue about it anymore."

She agrees. We move on.

Renting a car and driving from LAX is very familiar—we've done it dozens of times—but the fact that the car isn't headed to your house in Los Feliz guts me. It's exactly why I didn't want to come here.

The hotel is downtown, right across the street from the venue, and all the streets are shut down for blocks in preparation for the event. When we check in, they hand us a fat envelope with our itinerary and tickets to both the awards ceremony and the Governor's Ball. The tickets are gilded and beautiful. This is another world.

We check in and get dressed for the pre-party. It feels wrong driving up to the party in a rental Altima. There are paparazzi hovering outside. We walk up a short flight of stairs to long folding tables where NBC staff is checking people in. Our names are crossed off the list, and we head past security into the party. It is painfully loud. The music is pulsing and deafening. I have to shout to communicate with Mom, who is standing directly in front of me. It's also hard to find anywhere to sit or stand. The place is packed with beautiful people in beautiful clothing who are schmoozing, kissing cheeks, and throwing their heads back in laughter. I have to turn sideways and squeeze in between people and their conversations to get from Point A to Point B. Point B is the sushi bar, where two men are preparing fresh hand rolls. I'm starving and would love a fresh hand roll. I grab a cocktail off a tray and make my way into the line. After the sushi bar, we squeeze over to the raw bar that's overflowing with shrimp, oysters, and crab legs. I note how much you would love the food here but likely hate the party overall. This is not your scene. You would be the only one in a hoodie.

I turn to Mom and say, "No wonder he became a drug addict."

We run into a few people from *Parks* and make small talk. Most of the evening is spent with Aisha Muhharar and her Jewish boyfriend, Ben. I'm grateful for the opportunity to finally meet her after hearing so much about her over the years. They manage to snag a table, and we sit and talk forever, mostly about Ben being great marriage material because of the Jew thing. We are biased.

I see why Aisha was one of your best friends in the *Parks* writers' room. Like you, she is so down to earth and human. Conversation is effortless, despite the fact that we're screaming at each other from across the table. It really is obscenely loud, and her boyfriend happens to have hearing loss (did you know that?) for which he recently got a formal evaluation and will soon be fit for hearing aids, so we talk all about that. He pulls up his audiogram, and I compare it to Iris's, which I also happen to have on my phone. It's rare for both of us to find someone else who knows how to interpret an audiogram. Instant bonding material.

After the party, we meet our childhood friend Johnny for ramen at Daikokuya in Little Tokyo. That was always your favorite place to take us when we were in town even though it was always mildly stressful because you were so impatient, and there's only like five tables in the restaurant, and you have to put your name on the list and wait outside for at least an hour to be seated and you would smoke and pace so much it sort of soured the meal once we finally got to it. We would both get the tonkotsu ramen with the side of chicken fried rice. The Best. The broth is creamy; the noodles homemade. I crave it for months on end in the winter—and the summer, too. Year-round, really.

The last time we were at Daikokuya together was the first weekend you met Mike. It was spring break 2012. He and I stayed at your house. We went to that bar in Los Feliz and met up with Johnny and Taal, who—as we both know—has been struggling to find his way for a while but is having an even harder time now that you're gone. You were probably his closest friend in the world, and he's lost without you. Anyway, Johnny took one of my favorite all-time photos of us in the tiny waiting area of the restaurant that night. It's been my Facebook cover photo for months now. We're sitting there together with a space between us. There's Japanese writing on the wall behind us. I'm looking down at my phone. You're wearing a white T-shirt and a black hoodie. Your arms are crossed. You're looking off in my direction with a satisfied grin and this unusually peaceful look on your face. I love this photo of us.

Mom and I put our name on the list and wait for Johnny outside. He was Jonathan when we were growing up, but now he's Johnny. He was cool and funny in high school, but now he has a tattoo of a Tim Burton heart over his actual heart, and he's getting art-world famous with his surreal, mostly pornographic, collages on Instagram. He sent us two framed prints for the new house. They are so cool. You would love them.

Johnny gets out of his Uber *druuunk*. The three of us squeeze onto a tiny bench, and he smokes a cigarette. I want one so badly in that way that you want to do what you always used to do with certain people. But I haven't smoked a cigarette since 2007, and I'm certain if I smoke one now, I won't ever be able to stop because life is so fucking hard, and I have a baby, and who wants to smoke around a baby? I love that joke you used to tell about that, about smokers justifying their smoking. Like, "Well, I'm in the car, so I should smoke. Or, I just smoked a cigarette, so I should smoke another cigarette. Or, *oh*, I'm around a baby, I should smoke a cigarette!" You would kill me if you were able to see how severely I just butchered that goddamn joke.

Johnny is exactly the medicine that Mom and I need. He has always made us—including you—laugh until we're unable to breathe, the best kind of laughter. We eat ramen and drink beer and laugh obnoxiously loud and talk about sex (*Johnny's sex*) and watch videos of Iris and cry about you and eventually head back to our hotel where we order up a cot for Johnny, take selfies, and stay up giggling slumber-party style into the a.m. hours.

The next morning, after a nice brunch with my in-laws, who live in LA, I find a hair app called Blow Me and arrange for a stylist to come straighten my hair in the hotel room. We get dressed. I put on mascara for the occasion and sparkly, dangling earrings that belong to Mom. My shoes hurt before I even leave the hotel room, and I know my heels will be bloody within hours. All of this is your fault.

Around three o'clock, we head out. It's hotter than usual in LA today, and we have to stand directly in the sun in a very long line to get past the gates and security stations. Once we get to the front of the line, we take a photo next to the iconic gold statue that we can post online. The red-carpeted pathway on which we walk is parallel to the *real* red carpet with all the A-list celebrities, but there are so many photographers lined up along the sidelines that it's hard to see what's going on. It's yet another very crowded event full of beautiful people in beautiful clothing. How did you do all this? (Drugs.)

Once we get into the lobby, it's even more congested. We find ourselves stuck in a clump taking synchronized baby steps to get into the theater. Jon Stewart is standing right beside me. He's very short. I am ever-so-slightly starstruck. It's Jon Stewart. Of *The Daily Show*. (!!!)

We find our seats in the center section, next to the *Parks and Rec* people. I notice that I'm two rows behind Mandy Patinkin. This is a huge deal, as I have an irrational crush on Mandy Patinkin. Not the young one—the current one. He basically looks like how I imagine Mike will look in thirty years so, really, I have a crush on an older version of my husband. I snap numerous stalker-style pictures of him over the course of the night and post one on Instagram during the show, which drags on for hours. Tina Fey is standing in the aisle at the end of our row chit-chatting with Mike Schur, your boss and show-runner of *Parks*. The *Orange Is the New Black* ladies shuffle down the aisle quickly like giggly teenage girls to get to their seats before the show starts. They look stunning without the beige jumpsuits and face tattoos. And then, it happens. I spot Coach Taylor, which is basically like spotting the president! I get that I'm referring to a fictional character, but *Friday Night Lights* is our favorite show of all time, and this is a huge, *huge* fucking deal.

Remember when you sent me the full *Friday Night Lights* box set a few years back, before it came out for public consumption, and you taped that index card to the front and wrote *Clear Eyes Full Hearts Can't Lose* in blue Sharpie? It's still taped to my desk at work, next to years of neon Post-it notes from students that say *U R Snapchat Famous* and *Your bebe is CUTE!* and *Should I go to college?* One student wrote a Post-it recently that said, *They say you should dance like nobody's watching but really you should dance like everyone is watching so you will dance better.* It takes me weeks to realize that this was a quote from one of your Vines. They quote you all the time. I want to text you so badly in this moment and say, *OMG, I'm in the same room with Coach!!* But I can't. That is why I'm here.

Since the event is live, we are only allowed to get up and move around during commercial breaks, and in those commercial breaks, chaos erupts. Everyone is up and schmoozing and buzzing around the room. There's a big digital clock on giant flat screens on either side of the stage counting down the minutes and seconds until the end of the break. I leave to use the restroom and get a bottle of water thirty minutes in and a seat-filler takes my place. I was desert-level thirsty when we came in after the long line and the blazing sun and the clump of people in ball gowns, but they closed down the beverage station thirty minutes before the ceremony even started to get butts in seats for the big opening number. I saw Penelope Ann Miller try to sneak under the ropes only to be chastised by the man monitoring the bar and sent back from whence she came. The bar reopened once the show started, thus saving me from dropping dead of dehydration.

There are free tubs of fancy red lipstick next to every sink on the bathroom counter. I take one even though I don't wear lipstick because it's free. I put it on and look like a little girl playing dress up. I wet a paper towel and wipe most of it off before heading back into the theater. Jeffrey Tambor is accepting his award for *Transparent*. Were you alive to see this show? God, it's good. You would love it.

My heart starts pounding during the segment before the In Memoriam segment. The screen displays a warning that it's coming up next. Then the lights go dim, and Mom fetches Kleenex out of her purse. We grab hands tightly. The room falls silent. Your picture flashes on the screen for several moments with the caption *Harris Wittels, Writer/Producer*. It's a shot of you playing Harris, the animal-control guy, on *Parks*. You're wearing a flannel over a purple Phish T-shirt with a rainbow logo. Your head is in a vise. It's the weirdest photo in the bunch. Mom and I cry. The people around us cry. When the slide show is over, the boisterous, bustling crowd is completely still, reverent and quiet. The whole room is focused on honoring those who have recently passed. You are the youngest one by several decades.

*Parks* loses Best Comedy series to *Veep,* which is bullshit. I mean, it was a likely conclusion but still disappointing. No one is particularly bummed about it. I guess it's just how it goes. But it would have been nice to win, since the show just wrapped forever and one of the executive producers was just featured in the In Memoriam with his head in a vise.

After the awards ceremony, which takes a short lifetime, the entire auditorium at the Microsoft Theater files out of the same three side doors and walks in a herd to the Governor's Ball at the convention center across the street. It is like walking into magic or the most expensive wedding reception I've ever seen. Thousands of twinkling lights hang from floor to ceiling. A huge, layered stage is in the center of the room like a gigantic cake with a band on top. Pink and magenta lights shine into every corner. Massive, white floral arrangements sit on every table. Every inch is dripping with money.

Right when we enter, we are greeted warmly by the woman you were dating on and off during the year leading up to your death. The one who came after Sarah. She's a talent agent, which is why she's here. We know her because she's Jewish and from Houston, so we're basically from the same tribe. You actually went on your first date when you were home last Christmas break—I remember how skeptical you were but how much fun you ultimately had. I don't know why it didn't work out between you two. Well, I do. Heroin. I know that you went to her house the night before you died and begged her to let you inside, to give it another shot. But she was already dating someone else by then, and your last-ditch effort failed. Yet another shame. She was a good one.

After hugs and goodbyes, we head to our table: 420, your birthday, the birthday of Hitler, and the National Day of Weed. We sit down with the *Parks* producers. Everyone swears they had nothing to do with the table number. Of all the numbers in the room, we are all randomly seated at 420? It's a sign. It has to be a sign. (You did this, right?)

After a few minutes, we track down Amy Poehler and Mike Schur. Amy grabs us and squeezes us tightly. I remember when we first met her. It must have been 2010. Mom and I were visiting you in LA, and you were shooting a scene at some bar that would be the Snakehole

Lounge in Pawnee, the fictitious Indiana town where the show takes place. At some point, the actors went on a short break, and Amy and Rashida Jones rushed over to meet Mom and me. They were both eating bags of potato chips. Amy was like, "Oh my gosh, is this your family?! We love him so much!" She embraced us both with enormous hugs. She asked what I did, and I told her I taught middle-school theater (which was true at the time), to which she responded, "I loved doing theater in school! What are you working on?" Mom jumped right in and responded, "She just directed *The Importance of Being Earnest* and she won first place at UIL!" This was just the most Mom moment. As if Amy Poehler gives a shit about my stupid middle-school drama competition. But you sure would have thought I'd said I was the president of the United States. Both of them were so excited about it. "Wow, that's amazing!" When a production person came to pull them back to set to shoot the next scene, they apologized to us for having to go.

You always said *Parks* was the nicest set in Hollywood, and I learned then that it was true. These were normal, nice people. I'm glad that they were the people with whom you surrounded yourself on a daily basis.

That whole trip was so much fun. We got a real glimpse into your world. You had your own reserved parking space with the *Parks* logo and your name printed on it. For some reason, this stood out as being particularly impressive to me. We visited all the different locations on set. I took photos on Anne's couch, at Leslie's desk, in Ron's office. It was delightful to hang out in Pawnee for a little while. That night, we went to a great little Italian restaurant with Mom, Johnny, and Taal. We ate and drank and laughed until our stomachs hurt. It was a perfect day and night. I would give anything to be here in LA right now with you still in it.

Now, standing there in our fancies, I tell Amy I chose her book, *Yes, Please*, for our summer reading assignment at school—it's one of the many books I took from your bookshelves when we cleaned out your house back in February. You were always a voracious reader. The kids loved the book, obviously. I tell Amy that one of my students in particular is obsessed with her to the point of a restraining order. He was so excited that I was coming here and that I might possibly get to see *her*. She grabs my arm and says, "Ooh, let's make him a video!"

We all head to an area of the room with more light. Mike Schur takes my iPhone and starts recording. He directs me to announce Amy casually, and then he'll pan over to her for the surprise effect. (Is he really this great of a guy?) So I say, "Hey Nathan, I just have someone here who wants to say hi to you!" Then the camera pans to Amy. "Hi Nathan! It's Amy Poehler. I hear that you like my work, and I know that I like yours even though I haven't met you. So, I just wanted to say, Happy September, keep on being yourself, you seem really cool, and I hope meet you some day. Bye!"

Despite my initial dread and hesitation, it really couldn't be a lovelier evening. The show has come to an end. We are here to honor you. We are here to celebrate your work with all the people who sat in a room with you every day for the last five years. This has nothing to do with heroin or death or tragedy. We aren't sad or angry or resentful. We're just proud. We are so proud of you, Harris.

At around midnight, I walk back to the hotel, barefoot, holding my shoes in one hand and Mom's hand in the other.

# 19

---

## Seven Months, Four Days

We all do this differently. Some people find comfort in visiting graves. Others don't. I go on milestones—birthday, death day, etc. Mom never goes. Dad has been going by himself nearly every Sunday, though he still can't say the words. He just says he's going to "the office." The first time we visit the cemetery as a family is on Yom Kippur, the Day of Atonement, nearly seven months after the funeral.

On this, the holiest day of the year, we are mostly quiet. We feel our feelings independent of one another. Dad walks away and sits on a bench in silence. At one point, I join him, laying my head on his shoulder. I'm not sure he even notices me there. This is killing Dad. He's seventy-three years old, and every passing day, he seems to move a little slower and grow a little weaker. I think it may actually be killing him.

After the cemetery, we head to synagogue for the afternoon service. We'd debated whether we even wanted to go this year. There will be so many people to face who will be looking at us with pity, as people now do. We decide to go to one service, Mom's favorite, the contemporary service, A Confession for Our Time.

When we arrive, the only seats available are on the far sides of the chapel next to the plaques of congregants' names who have passed away. Each name has a small, round light next to it that lights up the week of their Yahrzeit, or anniversary of their death. All of them are lit up for this holiest of days. The cavernous sanctuary must seat a thousand people, yet we happen to sit on the aisle directly next to your plaque: Harris Lee Wittels. There it is. In plaque form. Another permanent record. Seeing it sends Mom into a fit of hysterical sobbing. Her friends swarm around her like bees. The service starts shortly after, so she hasn't fully recovered when everyone takes their seat.

Much of the service focuses on the ways a person has failed over the year: individually, as part of a family, as a member of society. The rabbi spends a good deal of time talking about the relationship between parent and child. He implores us to admit our shortcomings and decide to do better next year. You don't have this option, so the whole thing feels like a masochistic exercise. I worried that this would be too much for Mom. She cries through this service every year, dead son or not. I whisper in her ear that we don't have to stay. We can leave at any point. All she has to do is say the word.

It's four o'clock when we sneak out of the sanctuary and step into the sunlight. Not yet sundown, so technically not time to break the fast, but in light of our shitty circumstances, we assume God will understand. We get in the car and head to pick up Iris from school together, a rare, and thrilling, occasion for her. When Mommy, Daddy, Bapa, and Momo walk through the door to Iris's little classroom, she doesn't know who to run to first. To her, this is a special day.

To break our fast (well, for Mom, Dad, and Mike to break their fast—like you, I *never* fast), we head to a new pizza restaurant down the street that pales in comparison to Star Pizza. Dad and I order a bottle of wine. Iris is enamored with the fire in the brick oven. She thinks it's a giant birthday candle and sings the happy birthday song at least a dozen times. As we shovel appetizers into our mouths, Mom mentions her upcoming trip to Washington, DC. She'll be attending a rally in a couple of weeks called the Unite to Face Addiction summit. They're doing a comedy showcase in honor of you and comic Greg Giraldo, who also died of a heroin overdose. A comedy showcase at an addiction rally seems like an odd mix, but Tig Notaro is slated to perform, and she managed to make a recent cancer diagnosis funny. So maybe it will be funny? Quick editorial on Tig: I love her. She's reached out several times since you died to check on us. A bona fide mensch. You had such wonderful friends.

Anyway, the organizers of the event read a piece I'd written about you a few months back and sent me an invitation to attend and speak at the comedy showcase. No part of me wanted to do this, so I passed the info along to Mom, who is eager to carry the torch. She wants to do the outreach and fight the battle and be involved.

This is nothing new. She's always been involved. Growing up, she was a stay-at-home mom who was always available to pick us up for orthodontist appointments and sick days. She always kept the fridge and pantry stocked. She was always there when kids needed help—any kids, us or others. In middle school, when Chloe was incessantly fighting with her dad, Mom took her in for three months, no questions asked. She packed her a sack lunch every day. In high school, when Johnny's mom, Grace, died from cancer, Mom all but legally adopted him.

Her primary role has always been Mom.

So, naturally, she's no longer herself. She still lights up around Iris, but that's about it. All her posts on Facebook are related to addiction, loss, grief, and isolation. It's a whole other heartache to see her this way, this charming Southern lady who once glowed with her *honeys* and *sugars* and *darlins* and silver hair and green eyes and perfectly painted lips and ageless skin. It's hard to see your mother in pain.

Iris is always bringing me *Frozen* Band-Aids to cover my owies. I have this teeny, tiny red dot on my knee that's always been there, and Iris fixates on it. She touches it and studies it and says with great concern, "Mama, owie! Wha happen, Mama?" She's so concerned with my being hurt. It's hard to see your mother in pain.

Mom never expected this to happen. She feared and worried and fretted and obsessed and lost weeks and months of sleep—she knew it *could* happen, but a mother never *expects* her child to die. A child is supposed to bury a parent. There's no way to prepare for the other way around. And now, where there used to be an innate buoyant light inside of her, a heaviness resides. A life sentence. The torture of waking up every morning and having to re-remember.

Plus, there's a palpable stigma attached to overdose, especially heroin, that's been hard for Mom to accept. It's not an honorable way to die, like being a war hero or the victim of a natural disaster. There's a hierarchy in death like there's a hierarchy in life. When someone dies of breast cancer, no one questions where her parents went wrong. Sick people are victims; drug addicts aren't. No one's going on the internet and bashing a cancer patient for dying. One death feels out of a person's control while the other feels like a choice—a very shameful choice. Although Mom has been spared complete and utter *shame* since you were "famous."

"He wasn't the stereotypical drug addict living under a bridge or in jail or stealing from his family," she told me recently. "People revered him and honored him. No one looked at him and said his parents failed him. He was a high-class, functioning drug addict."

Status is very important to Southern women.

Mom is very active and involved in her grief. She initially went to grief therapy and cried and screamed and pounded the floor—*literally*—until she dug down deep and had nothing left to say. The grief counselor put her in a support group for people whose loved ones committed suicide, but she couldn't relate to that strain of tragedy. She felt different with her scarlet letter O, for overdose. She found a support group on Facebook called GRASP, which stands for *Grief Recovery After a Substance Passing*, where grieving mothers and other family members post photos and statuses all day long about the children they've lost, primarily to heroin. They post articles titled "Heroin in the Heartland" and "Breaking Point: Heroin in America." They share quotes in script, surrounded by backgrounds of open sky, that read, "Your wings were ready, but my heart was not," or "Those we have held in our arms for a little while, we hold in our hearts forever." GRASP is the saddest place I've ever been.

The only place sadder is in the eyes of our father. He has no online support group. He doesn't even know how to use the internet. Completely alone in his grief, he hasn't talked to anyone since you died—not a therapist, not a friend, not a wife, not a daughter.

A few years back, you did an interview with *Serial Optimist* where you said Dad was "the funniest dude alive." And he was. Remember when he knocked out his two front teeth attempting to play a harmonica and had to wear that retainer with two false teeth attached to the front? He would always take it out at restaurants and put it in other people's water glasses. He ate from dessert trays as waiters described daily specials and took musicians' violins out of their hands to badly serenade dinner patrons. When we were teenagers, he tried his hand at stand-up comedy at the Laff Stop open mic. A doctor by day, he called himself Dr. RIP and had that one terrible prop bit where he glued a dildo on a cereal box of Kix and made some joke about getting your kicks.

Your comedy career filled him with immense pride. He went into medicine but always secretly wanted to do what you did and was able to live vicariously through you. Whenever he saw you in person or spoke to you on the phone, he'd always run down his laundry list of show ideas, joke ideas, script ideas, and book ideas. He had so many ideas.

He's no longer full of ideas. No longer funny. No longer alive. I hate you for doing this to him.

The night after our Yom Kippur cemetery family outing, Dad comes over to babysit Iris for a couple of hours. After putting her down for bed, I trap him into having a conversation—just the two of us. Sippy cup in hand, I head downstairs to find him slumped down, feet on the coffee table, remote control glued to his hand. He's still in his work clothes that hang off him now because he's lost so much weight. For his birthday in July, I bought him new jeans that are two sizes smaller, but even those are too big now.

It's not the first time I've seen him this way—ransacked and vacant. This Yom Kippur, it's because of you. Twenty years ago, it was because of me.

When I was fifteen, I fell hard for a boy. Let's call him Ben. He was so cool. I only had my learner's permit, but he knew how to drive. He drove a hand-me-down Chevy Monte Carlo with velvety seats. He played in a band and smoked tons of weed. I don't recall him being particularly nice. I don't recall him being anything definitive at all really. No matter. I loved him ferociously, and it consumed me.

Dad hated him, of course, which only made me love him more.

One afternoon while Mom and Dad atoned for their sins at Yom Kippur services, I had sex with Ben in my childhood bedroom, under a ceiling of glow-in-the-dark stars.

I'm not sure where you were that day.

I remember being too scared to walk into the pharmacy and buy the pregnancy test, so Ben drove us to our favorite diner to kill time. I ordered my usual chicken tenders basket with fries but couldn't eat a bite because my stomach ached with the knowledge that I was in very serious—very adult—trouble. More trouble than I knew how to handle. I didn't need a test to tell me that. My sore and swollen boobs were evidence enough.

Ben's parents happened to be out of town that weekend, so we took the pregnancy test to his house, where I locked myself in the hall bathroom. My chest was clenched; my pulse, explosive. When I read the results, I fell to the ground, hitting my head on the counter on the way down.

I felt numb, empty, panicked, terrified, ashamed, sad, mad, and bad. Very, very bad. That night, we drank a 40-ounce of malt liquor in Ben's backyard.

The next few days were profoundly heavy. It was the first time in my life I'd felt that kind of weight. While all my friends worried about an upcoming geometry test, I worried about how I would tell Mom and Dad I was pregnant.

Aside from the teen sex, drug experimentation, and cigarette smoking, I wasn't a bad kid. I got good grades, had passions and interests, went to a competitive, specialized high school for performing arts. Teachers always gave me the highest marks in conduct. *I wasn't a bad kid.* I was a good kid who did a stupid thing. But getting pregnant at fifteen and having to deal with the emotional trauma, stigma, and shame of having an abortion taught me very early on that my actions do, in fact, have consequences. A leads to B, which leads to C, and C can sometimes really suck:

I have unsafe sex, I get pregnant, Mom weeps an ocean of tears and threatens to send me to boarding school.

I have unsafe sex, I get pregnant, I'm taken to a doctor the day after telling my parents and forced to look at the doctor's kids' baby pictures that sit on top of his desk while he makes sure I understand my options.

I have unsafe sex, I get pregnant, a nurse puts a mask over my face, a tear spills down the side of my face and onto the operating table as I drift off to sleep staring at a computerized sonogram image of a baby inside of me who I'll never know. When I wake up, full of lead, a Depo-Provera shot is being administered in my ass and an HIV blood test is being shot into my arm.

I have unsafe sex, I get pregnant, Dad doesn't speak to me for a solid month. No *good morning, how was school today, pass the salt*—nothing. I'm an invisible ghost who floats around the house haunting my loved ones. An invisible ghost who hates herself and will continue to hate herself for years to come.

Like most traumatic events, this ordeal had a tremendous impact on my future. Pretty much immediately after it happened, I developed this obsessive need to prove that I was "good." I didn't want to upset Mom and Dad any more than I already had, so I chose to be the very best version of myself. I spent hours every night doing my homework, stopped taking acid every weekend, auditioned for every school play and got leading roles, pulled back from the shitty boyfriend. From there:

I went on to graduate seventeenth in my high school class.

I attended New York University's Tisch School of the Arts and graduated with honors.

I got a master's degree in theater education.

I spent ten years teaching at exceptional schools and cultivating relationships with hundreds of phenomenal students.

I married a wonderful man who is nothing like my shitty, teenage boyfriend. He is extraordinarily nice to me. He is also creative and inventive and funny and patient and wise and supportive and thoughtful and kind. He and I chose to have a child, and now I am a mother.

I gave birth to a magnificent daughter. She is my everything.


Things turned out okay for me, Harris. Maybe if you'd had a uterus and got pregnant at fifteen, you'd have also learned that actions have consequences and ultimately not stuck needles into your arms.

Dad wears the same face now that he wore back then: expressionless but radiating sadness. When I was a little girl, I would wait and wait at the back door for him to come home from work, and when the knob turned, it was the happiest moment of my day. Where is that man? Is he still in there somewhere or gone forever?

I want to snap him out of it somehow, to say the thing that will make him realize it's not his fault, that he didn't make his teen daughter pregnant or his grown son OD. I want to take his hand, walk him out to the car, put him in the passenger seat, drive him to a really good therapist, and sit there with him until his mind is fixed. I want to fly him out to a sweat lodge in the middle of the desert where a shaman can lead him through an intense guided meditation that will exorcize the demons and make him realize he deserves to keep on living.

Instead, I ask if we can talk. He sort of sighs, turns off Fox News, and says, "Okay, let's talk." I miss our collective political war with Dad. He always loved to egg us on and spar with his "liberal, commie" offspring. I sometimes think he's actually a secret liberal who had a master plan all along to make his children liberal by pretending he believed the opposite. Now Mike and I are left to carry the commie torch, and it's not as fun without you.

Dad avoids eye contact and talks softly, almost in a growl. It's hard to know where to start. There's so much to say.

"Dad, I'm worried about you. How are you not talking about this? I don't understand."

"What's there to talk about?"

"Um, how devastated and sad you are?"

"I already know that. What do I want to talk to somebody about that for?"

"So you can stop blaming yourself?"

"Eh, it doesn't happen that way."

"So, what, you feel like you didn't do enough to prevent it?"

"We should have had a better relationship."

"Like from the beginning?"

"Yeah, from the beginning." He pauses and reaches into his memory. "I was always too busy—working all the time. I remember we went on this camping trip one time. He'd come home from Camp Blue Star one summer, and they'd gone camping while he was there, and he was excited about it. So we decided we'd go camping together one weekend, and we went and swam a little bit and ate but wound up coming home early the next morning." His voice trails off. "It just didn't turn out to be fun like he thought it was gonna be."

"Dad, I don't think that's true. Your perception is off. We went on vacations. You did Little League. You did Pinewood Derby. It's not like you weren't involved. You were very involved."

This memory flashes in my mind of me driving our minivan when I was nine years old. We used to go to this dude ranch every year in Bandera, Texas, and I couldn't ride the horses to breakfast every morning like you could because I was allergic to them. But Dad didn't want me to feel left out, so he would let me sit on his lap in the minivan and drive it behind the trail ride. I loved driving that minivan.

"Do you still go to the cemetery?" I ask.

"Every Sunday."

"And do what?"

"Just stand there."

"Do you talk to him?"

"No. He's dead."

"So, you just stand there? Does it comfort you to be there?" I ask.

"No. I think it puts me in touch with how I feel about things."

"Which is—what?"

"Which is…which is…what it is."

He can't articulate it.

"Sad?"

"Of course, it's sad. For me, it doesn't get any better."

"It's the same amount of shitty as it was from Day One?"

"Yep."

I flash back to that first conversation after I found out you died, where we sat on the bench outside their building, and I broke the news between sobs. I don't remember how I said it. I just remember his face going blank and a tear falling out of his eye. It's like he's still stuck in that moment, permanently shell-shocked.

"We used to go to Meridian, Mississippi," he says, "And your mother used to film a lot of stuff there—she lost most of those films—but anyway, there's just all those people in the films, and such a significant number of them are dead now. Gone. That's the way things are. That's the way life is. You just don't expect to see it in a child."

"Of course not. It's a horrible tragedy."

"No question about that," he quickly adds.

"So, it's just sadness from here on out?"

"I just think the effort it would take is not worth it."

"That's bleak."

"I mean, your presence is a positive for me." he adds. "And I know it's a positive for your mother. And the baby. And Mike. I like Mike."

"Don't you think you should go to a therapist?" I've asked him this no less than ten times over the last several months, but the answer remains the same.

"No, I don't think I should go to a therapist," he says firmly.

"Just one session. What if I go with you?"

"Good lord, I'm not going, and you're not going with me."

"Dad, it is important to me that you continue to live."

"I am living."

"But there is a direct correlation to happiness and joy and life span, and like you said, this has been shitty and horrible, and our family went from four to three and, like, if we lost another person that would be horrible. We can't lose another person, Dad."

"You're not gonna lose anyone," he says in this way that brushes off everything I just said, and I start to cry.

"Would you please just go to one session?" I beg him.

"No."

It's a losing battle. I drop it.

*Silence.*

"Dad, why didn't you wanna go with us to LA?"

"Because I didn't wanna be there."

"You don't wanna be a part of anything," I say critically.

"No, I just didn't wanna go there and be in the house and see all the places and all that. I just didn't wanna do it."

"I just think you feel responsible. I wish you wouldn't feel responsible."

He sits forward as if he's tiring of the conversation.

"If you feel responsible, then, I should feel responsible—" I start to say, but he cuts me off sharply.

"No, no, no, no. That's the least true thing you've said. You were a kid helping a kid. You weren't his mother. You weren't his father. You were a close friend, but you weren't responsible for raising him. You were brother and sister. Very close, but you didn't raise your brother. I hope that doesn't upset you."

"I just feel like you're saying you didn't talk to him enough, and you didn't have a good relationship with him, but I talked to him a lot, and I had a relationship with him, and he still killed himself. That's what I'm saying, Dad. I don't think anybody could have changed that."

He considers this. "Well, that very well may be—"

"Harris wanted to be sober, but he just—I mean, I wish you coulda been there to hear the therapist from the sober living place. The British guy. He said they offered Harris a Vivitrol shot three times, and he turned it down every time. He never really said, 'Hey, I have a problem.'"

"No, he never did. You're right about that."

"And that has *nothing* to do with you."

"I don't know."

"It doesn't, Dad."

"Okay. Well, thank you, Freud."

"I want you to talk to me."

"Okay. Well, we talked. We had a good talk. Anything else you wanna talk about? I'm worn out. How much do I owe you for this session?"

"This one's free. I love you, Daddy."

The rally in Washington is in two weeks. Mom has made plans to go by herself; airfare and hotel are booked. Dad isn't on the reservation. I walk him to the door that night and ask once more if he'll reconsider and go. Once more, he says no.

But something happens on the eight-minute drive from our house to his. When he gets home, he asks her to book him a plane ticket.

## 20

—

## Before

November 2014

After leaving rehab number two, in Oregon, Harris started an outpatient program in LA, four days a week for three hours a day. I checked in with him regularly during those first few weeks, but as October passed, he responded less frequently to my texts. I knew what it felt like when he detached. The same thing happened the first time he got out of rehab. After a while, the check-ins and *doing greats* became less frequent. The response time between text messages grew longer. I would go days without hearing from him, sometimes weeks. Every once in a while he'd send a request for an Iris video, but that was about it.

In one text, he told me he planned to go see Phish two weekends in a row at the end of October. The last show would be in Vegas on Halloween. Not even out of rehab thirty days, which is such a vulnerable time, and he planned to go to a musical drug den where he'd taken copious amounts of drugs in the past to, as he explained, "just listen to the music." I begged him not to go—too many triggers and temptations—but he'd always done what he wanted to do, and this was no exception.

One time, he hosted an epic Fourth of July party at his house in

Los Feliz that culminated in an angry letter from the homeowners' association. In it, Manager Glenn explains:

> *It has come to our attention that you had a large crowd of guests in the front of your home on the 4th of July shooting off an arsenal of fireworks. In fact, the following day, there was a debris field in front of your property of spent shells, casings, and gun powder stains in the street. It is unfortunate that LAPD had to be called twice to control the situation and that a warning from the Post Patrol guard was also ignored for a party that did not disperse until 3 AM Friday with guests loitering in the front yard and street.*

Harris gave no fucks about this letter. In fact, he proudly posted it on Instagram like a badge of honor.

I wasn't sure if he planned to go to Phish this time around specifically to use drugs or if he would use drugs as a result of being back in that environment. Either way, it was a fucked-up, self-sabotagey thing to do, especially now that he'd been given an opportunity to play the role of Aziz's best friend on *Master of None*. It was a substantial acting role, which is what he always wanted. Acting was his big dream. He loved playing Harris, the animal control guy, on *Parks and Rec*, and he wanted more of that. So why not chase *that* high? Why rock the boat now?

It was November 6, 2014, a week after Harris's Halloween Phish binge. Our kitchen and living room were crowded with a dozen over-stuffed trash bags of hand-me-down baby clothes from a friend. I was sorting and folding them into piles on the living room floor when I got

EVERYTHING IS HORRIBLE AND WONDERFUL

a Facebook message from Harris's old college girlfriend, whom I'd neither seen nor spoken to in fifteen years. It was disorienting to see her name pop up. Even more disorienting is that she told me he was using heroin again and that he hadn't told anyone but her. She didn't know what to do, but she wanted to do something, so she reached out to me.

The life was instantly sucked out of my body. My face went flush, my heart pounded, my breath slowed.

I called Harris immediately, and he actually picked up the phone. While I was relieved to hear his voice and know he wasn't passed out or dead in a bathtub somewhere, I was unable to mask my anger as I recounted what she'd revealed. He brushed the whole thing off with a cavalier laugh that carried the weight of cheating on a diet and casually admitted, "Yeah, I relapsed at Phish, but it's no big deal. I'm back on track now. I'm talking to my sponsor. I'm on my way to a meeting right now. I'll call after the meeting. Don't worry."

He didn't call.

Later that night, I texted him a photo of Iris I'd taken earlier that day. She was sitting peacefully in a swing at the park across the street wearing a houndstooth pilot cap that we put on to keep her hearing aids in her ears, a teal furry jacket, black leggings, and the yellow moccasins we'd bought the summer before in Utah. In the photo, she's grinning from ear to ear. Her little dimple makes an indentation on her round, right cheek.

> I hope you are going to a meeting tonight. I hope you will look
> at your beautiful niece's face instead of putting a needle in
> your arm. I hope you will value the amazing opportunity you've
> been given on Aziz's show and go back to working the Twelve
> Steps in order to keep your role. I know you're the only one

who can precipitate change so I hope you will be honest with yourself and go back to what you know. You have to admit you have a problem and that you are powerless. Not that you fucked up and it's not a big deal and you can pop some pills and get yourself back on track. It has to start from within and you have to go to the support group. You mean the world to lots of people, Harris. I hope you will get the help you need.

He replied.

I'm going to hang with friends at UCB. I didn't do drugs today or yesterday and I'll keep not doing them.

I instantly responded.

I think we both know that's bullshit. Go to the meetings. Every day. That's how you'll keep not doing them. You can't do it alone.

*And then he actually typed:*

I only hear from everyone when I relapse.

I was seething.

Are you fucking kidding me?? I send you pictures and updates of Iris all the time. When you start using again, you stop responding. Look back at your texts. I am always there. Plus you literally told mom to leave you alone about the sobriety shit. So no one asks you about it so as not to rock the boat. But maybe we should more. Because clearly it's still an issue. It's very clear cut. Go to meetings, work the program, every day. When you stop, you relapse. If you could control your addiction yourself, you wouldn't keep using.

My last message was time-stamped 10:15 p.m. He neglected to respond until 3:37 a.m., when I got the following text:

Okay. Look I fucked up. There is such a thing as a brief relapse. It's called a 'slip.' I will stay on track til I see you Thanksgiving so here is my brotherly favor I'm asking... Please don't tell parents. Keep this a secret like when we were in high school. I truly do not want to do that to them. I will check in with you more regularly. But at least wait and see if I fuck up again before we go freaking out for real. I'm alive, I'm going to a meeting with my sponsor tomorrow. I will not be able to look dad in the eye if he finds out I slipped. I will cancel my flight home. Please do this for me.

Once again, my brother was putting me in the fucked-up position of keeping a secret that could potentially kill him. Plus, he was just so full of shit. I didn't believe a fucking thing he said anymore. But the most pathetic part was that *I did it*. I kept the fucking secret. If it had been an episode of *Intervention*, Jeff VanVonderen would've cut me down to size with those piercing, steely eyes of his and tell me I was enabling Harris and, thus, part of the problem. I hated both of us equally and didn't respond to his text.

He sent another one at 3:48 p.m. the next day.

Hi Steph. Just left a meeting and feel really good. Just letting you know. Confessed all my sins.

I responded.

I'm glad to hear that. I didn't tell Mom because honestly it will destroy her. She told me a few days ago she had a bad feeling that you were using again and that if you were, it was the last straw for her. I don't want to break her heart. Please go to meetings every day. Please.

**Harris:** What do you reckon that means? The last straw.

**Me:** That she won't be able to have a relationship with you anymore if you are using. No more contact—this is what she said. It's too painful for her.

**Harris:** Okay I'm gonna call her now to check in.

**Me:** Are you going to tell her?

**Harris:** No. I'm going to stay sober. I had a hiccup.

**Me:** Do you have a game plan for how to make that goal a reality?

He responded immediately.

Meeting a day. Three calls a day. Steps.

Two weeks later, Pete Holmes aired a two-hour "Totally Weird" podcast in which Harris talked openly *with the world* about his heroin addiction and "recovery." While I applauded his candor and could see from Twitter that he was inspiring the masses, it was infuriating to hear him talk about his sobriety when I knew he was using again. The whole thing made me sick.

As I listened to Harris tell his story, I had the bizarre experience of hearing things that I'd never heard before. Each new piece of information he revealed was like a tiny little stab to the heart with a scalpel. I knew he'd been keeping things from me since he started using, but it really blew my mind that I was hearing all of this for the first time alongside millions of strangers.

Harris wasn't the first addict I'd known and loved, so I was aware that deceit was part of the disease. One of my best friends from childhood died of a drug overdose ten years earlier—a mix of cocaine and heroin. He was only twenty-five at the time. His girlfriend, another good friend from high school, was also an addict. I distinctly remember her nodding off in the middle of conversations and being hesitant to let her stay over out of fear that she would steal something. Addicts lie. I guess I just hadn't put my brother in that box.

On the podcast, I learned a litany of new things about my brother.

1. He'd been going to dangerous parks in the middle of the night to score heroin.
2. He did this often.
3. He was robbed one night at one of these parks.
4. He called in sick from *Parks* for four days and sat at home alone, shooting heroin.
5. During this staycation, he had a "mini overdose."

He told Pete Holmes that Robin Williams had gone to the same Malibu rehab as him. He said it's sad when anyone dies, even though every single human dies, but that it's extra sad that the world doesn't have Robin Williams's comedy anymore.

"And it's sad for his family," he said.

Then he paused. And I could hear in that small silence that he thought about his family. He thought about Mom and Dad. He thought about how destroyed they'd be if they lost him.

"If I go out again now that it's shooting heroin, I could die. That's it. It's not fun anymore. It's life or death now. I don't want to do that to my parents. I don't want to do that to myself. Um. So I'm taking it more seriously now. And I'm in a good place."

# 21

—

# Eulogy

No one ever gets to hear his own eulogy. It's likely the most adoring thing anyone will ever say about us, and we never get to hear it.

Remember when we threw a funeral party for Dad's seventieth birthday, and everyone brought a eulogy to read aloud. It was dark, sure, but delightful. Much like Dad. You and I got on the mic and told our favorite "Dadisms:"

*"Sometimes you get the bear, and sometimes the bear gets you."*

*"The cemetery is full of indispensable people."*

*"Wake up and pee! The world is on fire!"*

*"Pussy pulls the freight train."*

That night, he got to hear how much everyone loved him. He's frugal with smiles but was beaming that night.

I keep thinking, maybe if you'd been able to hear the eulogy I delivered at your real funeral, you would've realized how much I loved you, and you wouldn't have done the thing you did. Maybe I could have saved you.

I said lots of things I'm sure I never said to you in any sort of earnest way.

Like:

"He made the rest of us look bad. He was the funniest. He was the coolest. He had the most creative, inventive, limitless mind that was perpetually working. He was never fully present in any single moment but always functioning on multiple levels—always thinking and revising, always surveying the room for new material, always typing a new joke on his iPhone or finger pecking furiously away on his laptop. He was a true and tremendous talent who accomplished more in thirty years than most people accomplish in a lifetime."

"He was loved for his comedic genius, yes, but people also admired who he was as a person. He was as raw, honest, and genuine as they come. And even though he could be exasperatingly stubborn, he didn't have a malicious bone in his body. He possessed an innate charm that drew people in. He was able to make everyone in the room feel like they were his best friend. He was kind and forgiving, generous and compassionate. He really seemed to give people the benefit of the doubt. He understood that on a basic level, we're all the same. We're all human, and we're all just doing the best we can. In his words: 'Let's stop finding a new witch of the week and burning them at the stake. We are all horrible and wonderful and figuring it out.'"

That was my favorite thing you ever said.

That is my favorite thing *anyone* has ever said.

And it was exactly you—horrible and wonderful and everything in between.

You used to love to come up to school and talk to my students when you were in town. They idolized you because you got paid to do comedy and said the word *fuck* a lot. And because you were so real and human and devoid of pretense, you made them think, "If he can do it, I can, too." You worked so hard but made it sound so effortless. I asked you once how kids who are interested in stand-up learn stand-up because I was teaching a comedy elective, despite the fact that I was not a comedian and had no prior experience. You said, "You watch stand-up and you write jokes and you get onstage a billion times and do it and learn what sucks and at first you imitate your idols and then find your own voice. The end."

The night you died, I got a text from a former student, an aspiring comedian whom you'd met several times over the years. It was so sweet—I wish I could have shared it with you. He said, "It was his example that made me believe it was really possible that I could make it in comedy, and he inspired me more and more as he continued to blossom as a writer-performer… Thank you for introducing me to him. And thank you for making me believe I could follow in that path. I owe the both of you for making me the person I am today, and I wish he could know that."

Did you not realize what you meant to people?

Everyone worshipped you, yet you still felt so alone. In the Pete Holmes podcast, Pete literally said to you: "Please feel loved in this reality." It sounds like a bullet point in a self-help book, but you didn't feel loved in this reality, and you certainly didn't love yourself. I think this was the root of the problem. You literally told me when you were home last December detoxing that you'd burned every bridge to the ground. It was such a ludicrous statement and so clear that it was coming from the darkest, most self-loathing, of places, one that was triggered by a severe dopamine drought in the brain. It also just wasn't true. You had body dysmorphia of the soul. I mean, maybe you'd pissed off an ex-girlfriend or two, but who doesn't have that on their resume?

Maybe it would've turned out differently had you heard all the beautiful things people said about you after you died. Maybe you would have finally understood how loved you actually were.

I'm going to tell you now.

The series finale of *Parks and Recreation* aired one week after you died and included a title card at the end of the show that read: *We love you, Harris.*

See? Loved.

Upright Citizens Brigade hosted a mind-blowing tribute show in your honor the week we were in LA packing up your house. It was such an emotional purge. Laughing and crying, crying and laughing. So many people and feelings and stories. My father-in-law babysat Iris at your house (she slept in your music room) so that Mom, Mike, and I could attend. When we arrived, everyone welcomed us with lovings. That was a word you liked to use. I think it works nicely here. Kulap

Vilaysack, Scott Aukerman's wife, led us to some couches in the front of the house that she'd reserved for us. Can I just take a moment to say that I love her? *I love her.* She is truly the greatest person. She still regularly texts and calls to check in. She helped us pack up your entire house the week after your funeral. She is the real deal: a superior and stellar human being who loved you very much. She and Jeff Ullrich, who founded the Earwolf podcast network with Scott, created these badass T-shirts in your honor that said *Motherfuckers just wanna laugh,* one of your most beloved quotes, sold them online, raised $25,000 in profits, and donated all of it to your scholarship fund.

I didn't know Jeff, but he reached out six months after you died to share some thoughts about you. In the email, he said, "I think I'm telling you this because I wish I could have told him." *Oh, I feel you, Jeff.* In this one section, he described a characteristic that so many people bring up when they talk about you: "In the same way people describe transcendent politicians, Harris made you feel like you were the only person in the room, and that what you thought mattered. He didn't care that you were a nobody podcasting entrepreneur (in 2010: what the fuck is a podcast?), and there were very famous people sitting eight feet away. He'd ask you questions, listen to your answers, agree, argue, take another drag of his smoke, and make a joke. I can't tell you how important that was to me."

Jeff also told me about this one very *Harris interaction* you had together at the SF Sketchfest in 2011. Now he's sober, but at the time, Jeff was drinking too much. He was there trying to launch Earwolf, and lots of important comedy people who could help make his dream a reality were hanging out at this one hotel bar. Knowing how important it was that he make a good impression, you pulled him outside for a cigarette and said, "Dude, I can't let you go back in there. There are tons of comedians and celebrities in there who you need to start podcasts with, but you are getting sloppy. Come with me to Jack in the Box, I'll buy you a burger." And you did! Then you put him in a cab and made him call it a night. He credits you with saving him from himself that night. As a posthumous thank-you, he recently took a trip out to Houston from LA *of his own volition* to talk to my students about how to be a podcast-network-creating bad ass. You couldn't talk to them anymore, so he did it for you.

See? Loved.

Anyway, the tribute show was packed. You should've seen it. There were literally five hundred people in the theater, and a line wrapped around the block. They had to stop selling tickets because the venue was at capacity. The show started at seven o'clock and didn't wind down until well after two in the morning with live music later in the night.

Your Sarah Silverman family got on stage first, which was apropos since this is where you got your start. They showed a heartbreaking slideshow created by your dear friend, Rob Schrab, of your days in their writers' room, on set, and beyond. A cover of Bright Eyes' "First Day of My Life," sung by Sarah and accompanied by your band, Don't Stop or We'll Die, underscored the video. You guys originally recorded it for Rob's wedding. The song was slow and sweet, even more poignant than the original version. The video was brutal. And beautiful. I sobbed. Everyone sobbed.

Sarah couldn't be there that night, but she hosted another tribute show a few days later at Largo, where she discovered you nine years before. Chelsea Peretti did a set straight from the depths of her soul. You seemed to drive her bananas, but she clearly loved you. (I think this is how most people who loved you felt.) Also, Jon Brion played. *Jon Brion, Harris!* You would have died. Again. Ha.

Sarah posted this series of tweets the night you died:

> **Sarah Silverman** ✓
> @SarahKSilverman                    🐦 Follow
>
> You should know that Harris was brilliant beyond compare. That his imagination was without limit. That he loved comedy more than anything.
> 8:33 PM · 19 Feb 2015
>
> ↩  ⇄ 1,503   ♥ 4,521

> **Sarah Silverman** ✓
> @SarahKSilverman                    🐦 Follow
>
> That his heart was big and he FELT hard. That he was someone who would reach out to tell you he was thinking of you for no particular reason
> 8:35 PM · 19 Feb 2015
>
> ↩  ⇄ 477   ♥ 2,602

> **Sarah Silverman** ✓
> @SarahKSilverman                    🐦 Follow
>
> That he was honest even if it was gonna piss u off or make him look shitty.  He told the truth. Even when it was ugly.  Even when he lied.
> 8:37 PM · 19 Feb 2015
>
> ↩  ⇄ 438   ♥ 2,404

Did you know she felt this way? That she loved you so much? She *truly* loved you. Sometimes, I scroll through Instagram and see a photo she's posted of you and her together, and it disorients me every time—like you two had been hanging out that day and took the photo then. But then I see lots of comments with multicolored heart and teardrop emojis and have to re-remember that you didn't.

Most of the *Parks and Rec* actors and writing staff got on stage to share their favorite Harris stories. There were dozens and dozens of them. They must've talked about you for close to an hour. Everyone had something to say. Most of the ladies' memories involved a marriage proposal from you to them. Amy Poehler looked right at Mom and thanked her directly for the gift of you. Mike Schur explained that you had "many passions. Most of them were pointless garbage." Then he and Joe Mande, another writer on the show, acted out a series of texts between you and Mike over the years, many of which related to Phish (pointless garbage) and many of which were completely ignored by Mike. Some favorites included:

**OCTOBER 26, 2012**

**Harris:** Dude sick Tweezer from Halloween 1990 show on XM 29. Then amazing segue from Foam into Fee, prob my fave set from pre-Rift era.

**Mike:** [silence]

**Harris:** Welp, take 'er easy!

**JULY 8, 2013**

**Harris:** Phish opened set two with "Energy" by Apples in Stereo. You like those guys, right? I'd never heard the song but it was enjoyable.

**Mike:** Get back to work.

**Harris:** Was this one of the most important texts you have ever received?

**Mike:** No.

**DECEMBER 29, 2013**

**Harris:** I'm backstage at Phish and all of Mike Gordon's family is raving about Parks and Rec to me. So I sincerely thank you from the bottom of my heart. Do you want me to request Sample in a Jar for you?

**Mike:** Glad for you. I kind of think we should ask Phish to be on the show, for the Unity Concert episode. They seem like they'd be into it.

**Harris:** The good news is I kiiiiinda maybe already floated it by their manager. He's into it.

**Mike:** So the "good news" is that you unilaterally acted on the show's behalf and made a major production decision for what might be the series finale?

**Harris:** That is correct, yes.

**Mike:** Oh Harris. Don't ever change.

**Harris:** Love ya bud!

**May 5, 2014**

**Harris:** Yawn, second time as the answer to a Jeopardy clue, no biggie.

**Mike:** [silence]

**MAY 14, 2014**

**Harris:** Just realized that Dr. Saperstein is the name of the OB-GYN in both our show and Rosemary's baby. Coincidence?

**Mike:** [silence]

**May 20, 2014**

**Harris:** Listen, you're better at symbolism and metaphor than I am. I'll give you a mountain bike if you watch the new Jake Gyllenhaal movie on demand and explain to me. It's called Enemy.

**Mike:** [silence]

**May 23, 2014**

**Harris:** Horny?

**Mike:** I desperately hope this wasn't meant for me and was sent accidentally.

**Harris:** Nope. 100% for you, friend. I was trying to build up as many unresponded-to texts as possible to show people at lunch next week cause it was getting funny to me.

**JULY 18, 2014**

**Harris:** I couldn't come in today because of butthole stuff. Went to a doctor. Just keepin' it trill with you.

**Mike:** "Butthole stuff?"

**Harris:** If you want me to get technical with you I can...

How did you keep a job? Mike was your boss. Truly astounding.

Matt Besser, one of the UCB co-founders, got up and read an incensed email from an audience member who had been deeply offended by "Badger's Promise," a weekly show that you and Armen used to do. The email-writer vowed to boycott the theater as a result. He hated it more than anything he had ever hated before in his entire life. Recounting the story brought a tremendous smile to Matt's face.

At some point, someone got up and read a letter from Louis C.K. I honestly can't remember who it was. Pieces of the night are blurry. Regardless, it was intense and sad and beautiful:

*Harris was a rare guy. He cared so much about his work and about comedy in general. He was a kind and wise kid. That's how I thought of him. A sweet, fucked-up kid. Always a little unshaven, always a bit of pervert in his smile, but such a decent chap, and he cared compulsively about you when he talked to you. I think he was so in touch with his own flaws and fears that he had sympathy for everyone.*

*I worried about him all the time. I didn't know if he had his shit together. I knew he felt too big in all directions. I knew life broke his heart every day. You could see that. I had lost touch with him in the last few years which I really regret now.*

*I had no idea he struggled so much with heroin. I have lost too many friends to heroin. I hate it. It makes me mad. But when I heard Harris was gone… What a horrible shock.*

Two weeks after you died, you were supposed to start shooting *Master of None*. Eric Wareheim ended up playing the role, which was based on you and originally named Harris. However, in true Hollywood fashion, you had to screen test to play yourself, which caused a fair amount of anxiety and stress. What if you didn't get the part of yourself? You were used to seeing things fall through—pilots, projects, etc.—but you *really* wanted this to work out. When they formally offered you the role, you were like Charlie from *Willy Wonka* getting your golden ticket. It was six days before you died.

This was the last project you would ever work on, but it was going to be the project that would catapult you into the next stage of your career. It was supposed to be a beginning, not an end. A few days after you died, Aziz sent me a long email sending his condolences. In it, he talked about what the show would mean for you:

I'm not sure how much he told you about the project we were working on together but he was the first person I wanted on board. He was fantastic. It was great seeing how much he'd grown as a writer and storyteller. He was a leader. He was hilarious. He challenged me in the best ways when everyone else was ready to move on. He was only there three days a week and we all hated those two days when he wasn't around. My little brother wrote on the show and loved him and Harris was like a mentor. He was so sweet to him and all the other younger writers.

The other week we cast him to play a part on the show and he was elated. I remember when we made the phone call that let him know he'd got the part, hearing the excitement in his voice now just makes my heart break. He was so excited and so were we. He was so thrilled to move to New York. He got a ridiculous haircut that he thought looked good. He was planning on losing weight and cutting back on his insane diet.

It was going to be *huge* for him.

I was so thrilled that more people were going to see his genius. It was going to be a raw, unfiltered version of his comedy that we just didn't have a chance to see yet. He was at the top of his game in so many ways. Knowing he was on the cusp of something so fantastic just adds another cruel layer of sadness to this whole thing.

I loved him dearly. We all did. And I'm so sorry he's gone. But the few years I had with him are better than 10,000 years with most of the boring people out there. I'm glad we all had him while we did. I'll make sure to keep him in my heart forever and everything I do will be in his honor with the goal of trying to make him laugh somewhere, wherever he is.

He loved you dearly, Harris.
Everyone did.
Wherever you are, I hope you know that now.

# 22

—

## Eight Months, Six Days

In ways, I always felt like your mother. It's not that our mother didn't do a good enough job or that we were latchkey kids or something like that—quite the opposite, in fact. I was just so proud of you in this way that—now that I'm a mother—can only be described as maternal. I loved you unconditionally from the start and always jumped at the opportunity to tell anyone who would listen just how special you were.

Today, Mike and I leave Iris with Mom and Dad and go to a play. Coincidentally, we sit next to two middle-aged women who are talking about Oddball Comedy Festival, which came through town last weekend. They're raving specifically about Aziz Ansari's set; how phenomenal, adorable, and hilarious he was. Aziz was kind enough to get Mike and me tickets to the show, but the baby wasn't feeling well. Or maybe I wasn't feeling well. Or maybe I just didn't want to sit there and see Aziz being funny and alive when you can't be either of those things.

In the old days, I would have boldly interrupted their conversation with "Oh, my brother is a writer and executive producer on *Parks and Rec*." I loved to brag about you and did it often. Not much to brag about now!

I mean, I could butt in and say: "You know, Aziz Ansari is a truly good person in real life. He sent us a churro cake in the mail. It was creamy and delicious. And he wrote the most beautiful tribute about my brother after he died of a heroin overdose. It made us all laugh after forty-eight hours of feeling like Mel Gibson in the torture scene from *Braveheart*. Aziz was a pallbearer at his funeral. My brother was a one of three writers on his new Netflix series that's being advertised every fucking place I look. Social media is a land mine—is that your experience of it? My brother was going to play Aziz's best friend in the show. It was going to be his big break into the acting world. He was moving to New York. He'd booked an Airbnb."

But you died, and none of that stuff happened. So I say nothing.

Watching *Master of None* is like sticking needles into a voodoo doll of myself, but I'm some sort of masochist and need to feel the pain. The goodness, originality, and authenticity of the show is mind-blowing. And you had so much to do with that. I hear your voice so clearly in it. Like that scene from the "Nashville" episode in which Aziz and his date are at a BBQ restaurant in Nashville, and Aziz is trying to negotiate what they'll split until he finds out she's a vegetarian. This is genuinely heartbreaking to him because it means no "splitsies." Splitting things was of paramount importance to you. One dish was never enough. You always had to try everything on the menu.

I think of our family vacation to Maui a few years ago. It was on this trip that you bought that blue Maui cap you always wore. Mom caught this scene on the flip camera you bought her for her birthday that year. It's one of the home movies in her collection.

We are seated at a large, round table covered in a crisp, white tablecloth. You and I are negotiating what we're going to order for dinner. Every meal we've ever had at a restaurant starts with a scene sort of like this. Ordering is always an epic ordeal that's plotted with the precision of a game of Risk.

Harris: "We should get a lobster dish and a red meat dish. And split 'em."

Me: "K."

Harris: "I say we get the lobster and the braised short ribs."

Me: "You don't want the steak special?"

Harris: "I'll also get—wait, there's a steak special?"

Dad: "Ribeye. With the bone in."

Harris: "Mom, will you trade seats with me cause I'm gonna share with Steph."

Me: "We could get the New York steak."

Harris: "That's boring."

Me: "Or short ribs are awesome. I'll totally get those."

Harris: "Yeah they're amazing."

Me: "Okay, so let's get the short ribs and the lobster, and I want the cake walk, too. You wanna split the cake walk?"

Harris: "No let's stick with our own appetizers."

Me: "But I kinda wanna get the buffalo tomato salad. Does that appeal to you at all?"

Harris: "We don't have to do that together."

Me: "But it's like a big stack."

Mom: "Just get your own buffalo tomatoes."

Harris: "It does sound pretty good. I'm gonna get the onion soup, too."

Me: "I wanted to try that."

Mom: "How are you guys gonna share?"

Harris grins.

Harris: "Mom, can we trade spots please?"

I always used to look for you in the credits of *Parks and Recreation*, *Eastbound & Down*, *The Sarah Silverman Program*, and other TV shows you worked on. When *Harris Wittels* flashed across the screen, my heart would light up and sparkle like some cartoon character and release a sort of chemical in my body that must be what parents feel like when their kid scores a winning touchdown.

When I see your name in the end credits of each episode of *Master of None*, I know it's the last time I'll ever see your name in this special place. So, it's a sort of suicide to hear Aziz and Alan Yang talk about the show on "Fresh Air" and in the *New York Times* and in *The Atlantic* and in *The New Yorker* and in *Salon* and on Twitter and on every fucking podcast and place on the internet.

But I want to watch the show for all the reasons I want to avoid it.

It's the last time I'll ever see your name in the ending credits of a great episode of television. It's the last time my heart will light up and sparkle in that way.

The last episode of *Master of None* included a title card that dedicated the series to you:

# 23

—

## Nine Months

It's both an honor and a punishment to be the person in charge of your estate. There's a lot of shit to notarize and fax and scan and fill out and keep track of and document and follow up with and put into piles and file in folders. And I'm terrible at filing. My skill set really ends at making piles. There are just so many things that need to get done in a timely manner. We weave a complicated web in our time here on earth, and untangling it amounts to copious forms to fill out and battles with fax machines and conversations with customer service reps that go like this: "I am calling because my brother died, and I need to close/cancel (fill in the blank)."

At first, these words were impossible to say; uttering them made it real, and I would inevitably break down and cry into the phone to a stranger working off a script. But I've said them so many times now that it's become entirely unemotional. When they say the obligatory, "I'm so sorry for your loss," I respond with a quick "thanks" and scurry on to the reason for my call. I'm certain they aren't sorry for my loss, so it's ever so slightly insulting. Plus, I just want to get on with it.

Per the instructions of your business manager, I go to a local Bank of America branch to close out your account. The guy who helps me has spiky, goopy black hair and wears a cheap, olive-colored suit that hangs on him oddly. He can't be a day over twenty-three. He is notably fidgety and energetic. It crosses my mind that maybe he just snorted a bump of cocaine off his house key in the employee bathroom. He is spinning his desk chair back and forth and drumming on the desk with his pen. We could have just as easily been talking about a concert we both attended. The whole conversation feels nauseatingly banal and irreverent. I am here to close my dead brother's bank accounts; he's doing another task at work.

Like most instances of closing a deceased person's account, there are numerous unnecessary hoops through which to jump. I'm convinced that institutions make it hard so you'll just say fuck it and leave all your shit there indefinitely. I was certain I had all the right things—a copy of the trust, an original death certificate, a warm smile—but this doesn't satisfy the needs of our banking institution. The guy calls some 800 number and asks the representative to guide him through what I assume must be a very common occurrence. After all, death comes to us all.

He pushes the buttons on his phone with the end of his pen and starts to play with the arm of the office chair as he holds for a representative. When someone picks up, he explains that the account holder died and then looks over at me while covering the receiver of the phone: "Are you his sister? One of his sisters."

"Yes."

He spins my driver's license around and around with his fingers on the desk.

"Oh really," he says into the phone. "Oh, my gosh. So, do we still have to send it through wealth management or can we just do that letter or whatever?"

Now he's snapping his fingers. *He's literally snapping.* He picks up the death certificate and starts reading portions of it out loud to the person on the other end.

"A letter of instruction or something like that?" He starts whistling. "*Mm-hmm, mm-hmm. Mmm-hmmmm.*"

I put my hand over my mouth because hateful sentiments are about to exorcist out of me, and I'm already late picking up Iris from school.

He hangs up with a chipper, "Thank you very much! Have a great day!" Turning to me, he says, "You have to complete a couple of forms, one for Texas and one for California, and then fax the wealth management department a notarized California Small Estate Affidavit."

"Where might I find such a document?"

"Google it."

I leave with a rage that seeps into the spaces between my bones and stays for the rest of the day and night.

This is how it is. I vacillate between bad days and days where I do a decent job of functioning in the real world. Despite the volcanic rage and profound sorrow that are now a part of my cellular makeup, I am very efficient. I take care of the things that need taking care of. I make jokes, post pictures of my kid online, attend parties, teach students, take daily walks pulling a little red wagon. I keep up with current events, have opinions, feel and express political outrage. I read the news, listen to *This American Life*, type emojis in text messages. I throw a housewarming party, direct another play, remember to give birthday gifts to my daughter's teachers. I'm convincing in my role. But when I catch a glimpse of myself in the mirror as I'm washing my hands or brushing my teeth, I see the outline of a mask. I don't look like myself anymore. Because underneath my skin, I'm miserable.

The dumb internet is partially to blame. I see your friends' lives moving on online. Proposals, weddings, babies. Things for which you would have been there. Things you'll never have the chance to do. These are the things that pile up inside of me.

And then, suddenly, it's eleven thirty on a Sunday night, and I'm standing in the bathroom in my underwear and a threadbare T-shirt that Harris used to wear, screaming about how bad it hurts. It comes out messy and guttural. I say *fuck* a hundred times. I melt into Mike's chest. I feel empty and hungover the next morning like I did when I woke up next to the toilet after my twenty-first birthday, when I drank too much tequila the night before and lost one of my favorite earrings in the subway.

This sort of explosion is becoming more rare as time passes, which is fortunate. It takes so much energy that there would be none left. Mostly, I'm learning to live with the feelings. It's all very normal now. I have curly brown hair. My allergies act up after I drink red wine. I had a little brother for thirty years. Now he's gone. When I do cry, it's quietly with the door closed. I know how to breathe through the sobs so only silent tears pour down my face.

It's not that I don't want to feel the feelings. I don't mind the feelings. I welcome them, in fact. I just don't have anything left to say about them. You're gone. You're never coming back. And it sucks. And it hurts. And it will always hurt. And that's just the way it is now.

## 24

—

## Nine Months, Six Days

Holidays are drone strikes: calculated and deadly. On the first Thanksgiving without you, Mom, Dad, Mike, Iris, and I fly to Phoenix to be with my in-laws. Mike's brother Jeff, his wife Hannah and their two girls, Sylvia and Judith, have all flown in from LA. So has my father-in-law, Steve. He and my mother-in-law, Ruth, divorced after Steve came out when Mike was thirteen years old, but they're still best friends who unite for most holidays and special occasions. It's very beautiful and inspiring and progressive and sort of like the TV show *Transparent*, minus the trans part. Ruth still lives in Scottsdale, where Mike's brother Dave and his wife Jenna recently bought a gigantic house. This is where we'll stay for the long weekend.

While I love them all, I quickly realize it's acutely painful to see Mike's brothers, their wives, and their children all under one roof. My nieces, whom I adore, remind me that I'll never have nieces or nephews who share my DNA. My mother-in-law and father-in-law have three grandchildren, including Iris, with two more on the way. Mom and Dad just have one.

Out in the world on any average sort of day, it's hard to hear people talking about their big families, multiple siblings, and the three, four, five, six, seven, eight grandchildren their parents have. It's hard to see photos of sprawling families communing by trees or in front of fireplaces wearing outfits in matching colors—partially because matching color schemes are absurd, but mostly because my family lost one member but shrunk an entire generation. I don't want to see anyone's happy fucking family, especially on a holiday. A holiday is the worst: an entire day built around togetherness.

But Thanksgiving is easier than I expect it to be, in large part because Iris is extremely sick. Vomiting, fever, rash, congestion, cough, generalized irritability. She's on her very worst behavior and leaving a trail of snotty tissues all over the house. I feel awful for her but realize in hindsight it's an excellent distraction. There's so much vomit to clean up, I have no energy left to feel sorry for myself.

It's weird—no one really mentions you over the course of the weekend and not at all on the Big Day. This happens on regular days, too, but it feels extra shitty on a holiday. And there's no green-bean casserole. You loved green-bean casserole. It was your favorite Thanksgiving dish. You used to make Mom prepare two every year so you could save an entire casserole for leftovers. I guess it's apropos that the dish is absent today too.

As I lie in bed that night, tears stream out of the corner of my eye onto my pillow.

"The whole point of the holidays is to be with your family, and a quarter of my family is dead," I say to Mike.

He tries to comfort me: "A quarter of your family isn't dead."

"A quarter of my *original* family is dead."

When we get home from Arizona, we put Iris on her second round of antibiotics for a double ear infection. She hates it. Twice a day for ten days, it's a two-man, pin-down job involving a sippy cup, a syringe, and a pacifier. Administering the meds tonight, I remember that time you basically claimed that antibiotics were some sort of sci-fi miracle antidote that boosted one's immune system for months at a time.

It was Christmas Day, 2004. It had snowed the night before, which was extremely unusual in Texas. I had gotten home to a room full of presents at 2:00 p.m., wearing the same clothes from the night before. Dad, who was super sick with some sort of upper-respiratory infection, made a passive-aggressive comment about how late it was or how Christmas gets later and later each year or something along those lines. Whatever it was, I took great offense because I was twenty-three and had the energy to take great offense to things.

"This isn't one of our better Christmases," Mom said.

I was in the kitchen building a giant lox sandwich, and all of you were sitting in the living room. Dad sat on the couch next to Mom with the blanket pulled up to his neck. You were filming all of this on the video camera.

"You're making it worse by making me feel guilty," I shouted from the kitchen.

Dad chimed in: "That's what mothers are supposed to do, Stephanie. Loving mothers make their children feel guilty."

"She's not making me feel guilty—you are."

"I am!?" His voice raised an octave. "What did I do!? I'm sitting here with a blanket over me. I'm dying. Ever since I quit smoking, my health has gone to hell. I better start smoking again just to save my life."

I laughed loudly. *This.* This was one of my favorite things about how our family functioned. Even in the midst of an argument, we could always break for a laugh.

"You should. It works for me," you said.

"Did you go outside to smoke last night in the middle of a snow storm?" Dad asked.

"Several times."

"That's unbelievable. You could have had pneumonia by now."

And then: "I took a Zithromax, like, two months ago. My white cells are through the roof."

Tonight, as I fight to get the medicine into my kid's mouth as she writhes on the ground like a piece of bacon in a frying pan, I think of your magical white blood cells.

And I laugh.

# 25
—

## Before

### November 2014

Two weeks after the Pete Holmes podcast aired, we expected Harris
to come home for Thanksgiving. It was the Tuesday before the holiday
weekend, and he was supposed to land in time for dinner. I assumed
he'd either want seafood or Mexican. I was already at work that morning when I got a text from my mom who copied and pasted a text she
had just gotten from Harris. No preface or explanation. Just this:

> Mom I love you and I'm sorry but I don't think I can come
> home. I had another relapse and was scared to tell you but
> I'm dealing with it and am just not in a place to come home
> and pretend everything is fine. I'm sorry I'm such a fuck-up.
> I really wanted to be with everyone. I'm not trying to hurt
> you guys. I'm so sorry.

I erupted into screaming sobs because there was now a volcano
where my heart should be. It was messy and hot and all over the place;
bubbly and sticky and oozing. It was also very uncomfortable for everyone in the office. They quickly vacated the room. I called my mom

and screamed into the phone: "What a fucking asshole! I knew he'd relapsed! I fucking hate him! What the fuck is wrong with him?! He ruins everything! He has destroyed our family. *Fuck him!*" This went on and on. Lots of *fucks*.

I worked at a school.

I was a raging bull. The togetherness I'd been loosely holding together all unraveled in this moment. I was so sick of his shit. Given the opportunity, I would've pummeled him and not stopped until I saw blood.

That night, my dad finally called Harris and asked if he wanted them to go out there to help him detox. Harris said yes. My dad said it would have to be Friday because they wanted to spend Iris's first Thanksgiving with us. I thought, "Yet another first that Harris is missing. Another holiday he's fucking up." The hate grew deeper.

This would be the first time in our entire lives that our family wouldn't be together for Thanksgiving. Harris would spend the day driving around LA with his drug dealer while his niece messily slurped up cranberry sauce for the first time.

Over the next few days, I purposely didn't reach out to my brother. I'd been angry at him plenty in the past, but in those moments of typical sibling tension I just yelled at him for a little while, he yelled back, and it was over. This felt heavier, more permanent.

However, as shitty as I felt about Harris's absence from Thanksgiving this year, I knew he felt a million times shittier. He was occupying the darkest space, sending texts like this to my mom:

> I got back on suboxone and just feel like crap.
> I miss you a lot. I hate this.
> It's my fault.

Mom confessed to him that her biggest fear was that her son was going to overdose whether he wanted to or not. Maybe he had a secret death wish. She said she was scared of losing her baby boy. He told her he wouldn't do that to her.

"No one ever overdoses on purpose," she said.

When my parents got to LA, my mom reported that Harris seemed empty, sad, and lonely. She cried a lot. The three of them spent a lot of time that weekend sitting in the dark with the curtains drawn, watching the giant television. My mom made a huge Thanksgiving dinner from scratch for Harris on Friday. He loved Thanksgiving food, and she loved him. She said he seemed grateful, as grateful as someone who was dead inside could be.

She also reported that Harris didn't seem to be in any physical pain or experiencing any symptoms of withdrawal. "The Suboxone must really be working," she concluded. My fear was that he wasn't detoxing at all. My fear was that he was shooting up while my parents slept down the hall in the guest room.

That weekend, he and my mom had a candid conversation outside on his back patio. He was smoking, as usual. My mom told him she was on a merry-go-round with him and didn't know if she could hang on for another relapse. It was killing her. "I'm an addict," he said. "I'm gonna relapse. That's what addicts do. But you're my mom. You'll always be there for me." It scared the shit out of her. He was basically saying he was going to relapse again and again and again. He already had. He was telling her he wasn't ever going to get better.

She begged him to come back to Houston and stay indefinitely.

She said he needed to get away from this place and clean himself up and be with his family. Harris said he wanted to come home but had to finish up *blah blah blah* thing first. Granted, he *was* busy. He'd done so well in his career up to this point because he was reliable and hardworking. And funny. Very funny. However, his career wasn't *our* priority—he was. He promised that when he wrapped things up in LA, he'd buy a one-way ticket home. It shouldn't be longer than a week or so. He wanted to come home. He was on board with our plan.

I wrote him a letter that weekend that still sits in the drafts folder of my email, a letter that said exactly how I felt. The truth. How angry, hurt, betrayed, sickened, scared, and anxious I was about him every minute of every day. How I was terrified he was going to die. How I wanted my brother back. But I got scared and sat on it. I didn't want to rock the boat. I didn't want to make him angry or push him farther away. I just wanted him to come home. I figured if we could get him home, maybe we could make him stay. Maybe we could look into his eyes or hand him the baby and inspire him to change. Maybe we could save him. Sometimes, I look at this letter and wonder if things would have turned out differently had I sent it.

# 26

---

## Nine Months, One Week, Four Days

I have an expansive digital record of our relationship for which I am grateful because my long-term memory is shit. When I type your name into my Gmail history, I can instantly pull up page after page of authentic samplings of you: your thought process, opinions, moments of weakness, moments of triumph, jokes, anecdotes, typos. I do it often.

I do it again when Aziz contacts me the first week of December about a piece he's writing for the *New York Times Magazine* called "The Lives They Lived." It's an annual In Memoriam, and they're going to honor you. His idea is to highlight some of the most Harris-ish digital interactions you had with the people to whom you were closest: texts, emails, chats, etc. There's so many from which to choose. You really shined electronically.

Our G-chats date back to 2007. Eight years of mostly meaningless and meandering conversations about girls (you) and boys (me); work drama; daily stressors; parents' birthday gifts; houses we should or shouldn't buy; dreams we had; nightmares, too. It's like a trunk of old letters buried in the backyard that I dig up, crack open, and spend hours exploring.

**Harris:** hey lemme run this thing by you

asked a girl out via facebook who we have a mutual friend,

but i've never met

she seems cute and funny

well here

im gonna cut and paste the convo

"ya id be down for that. always open for a nice chat. cant

this weekend going on a vacay haaaaay. maybe next week/

weekend. talk to you soon." — her

"Fuck off, it's this weekend or never. Just kidding. Talk to

you next week. Lookin forward to it and what not." — me

was the "fuck off" too strong? she hasnt responded

thought it was funny

**Me:** that's totally funny

**Harris:** ok cool

anyone would get it

**Me:** did you send it, like, an hour ago?

if she doesn't get it, she's an idiot and fuck her

**Harris:** word!

**Me:** ok so real quick tell me — are you in love?

**Harris:** i mean i dunno. its still nascent

but we are happy yes

**Me:** i can't believe you just used that word

but you feel like it's clicking?

good job on that word

**Harris:** it is clicking.

**Harris:** did i tell u i'm gonna be on the real world?

(We both loved *The Real World*, so this was a huge deal. This was a huge deal for both of us.)

**Me:** *What? No*
**Harris:** i talked to this girl at a bar all night and there were cameras on us and i signed a release form and she wouldn't tell me what it was for
and she gave me her phone number and told me to call the house tomorrow
and as she was leaving she whispered that it was the real world
so im gonna be the guy on the phone
and the guy in the bar
**Me:** *OMGOMGOMG*
**Harris:** and hopefully the guy in the night vision bedroom scene
**Me:** was she foine?
**Harris:** she was
they were doing their job thing
which was walking around with candy trays and trying to get tips and wearing these vests
for a group called the "meow meows"
and i said i'm in the ruff ruffs
and she giggled
and then she literally ripped my shirt off and put on her vest
and gave me the tray

**Me:** shut up!

**Harris:** and i started selling her candy

and getting a lot of tips

**Me:** That is fucking wild.

Were there sparks?

**Harris:** mad sparks

but i was wasted and on my A+ game

i was like whats yer name

and she was like kimberly

and i was like your last names burly?

she loved it

I need the digital record because my memories are unreliable. I worry that I won't be able to keep you alive in my mind over time. I can see the outline of memories in flashing images like a slide show. I have an idea about the theme of an interaction, but I couldn't write the scene. I couldn't take a lie detector test. I worry that my fragmented outline of memories will become even more barren with time.

What sticks out most vividly are your facial expressions:

Like the one where you squint your eyes and crinkle your nose and scrunch your shoulders up like you're hiding in your own face.

Or the one where you purse your lips tight into a pucker and raise your eyebrows.

Or the one where you have this totally blank, flat expression but there's so much going on behind the eyes.

I can picture you sitting in front of the TV at two in the morning, wearing flannel pajama pants, a Phish T-shirt, and a hoodie, watching *The Real World* or something equally inane and eating leftovers out of a Styrofoam to-go container with your fingers. You never used silverware.

I can see you sitting on the couch, one knee bent, finger-pecking furiously away on your laptop. You never learned to type properly but were lightning-fast on a keyboard. You could have won a competition.

These are the images I saw on repeat for thirty years. They're seared into my memory. Conversations are harder to conjure because they happened only once. I want to remember all of the things you said, but I can't. I can listen to podcasts or stand-up DVDs or Mom's home movies, but I can't remember all the things you said to me on the phone at two in the morning while freaking out about a girl, and I want to remember those moments so badly because they're all I have. We can't create any more memories.

For some reason, I can remember lots of times as teenagers when we got fucked-up together:

Like the time you picked mushrooms in a field after it rained, and we dehydrated them upstairs in the middle of the night in the food dehydrator Dad bought to make beef jerky. The whole upstairs smelled like cow shit for days. Mom and Dad didn't seem to notice. How?

Or the time we took acid in high school and hung out by the pool in my friend Nellie's backyard until six in the morning. You accidentally took a sip out of the Coke can that was full of cigarette ash and gagged for several minutes. We laughed about it until we cried for weeks, months, years. I still laugh when I think about it.

Or the time you came to visit me when I was a freshman at NYU. You were only a high school sophomore, a little boy, but we somehow got you into a bar down the street called the Fat Black Pussycat. A dark place coated with red velvet. You drank too much and threw up all night. But it was funny.

Or the time in middle school when you and your friends rolled fake joints out of oregano and brown paper lunch sacks and Mom found it the next day, woke us all up at seven in the morning, and dragged us out into the backyard to bust us for smoking pot. I told her it was oregano and that you were stupid and went back to bed.

Why do I remember this stuff?

Because you died of a drug overdose?

Because I have to somehow make myself responsible?

I remember other stuff, too.

Like how you loved to make Hungry Man frozen dinners at three o'clock in the morning in our old house on Dumfries.

Or when you played the title role in the musical *Oliver* in middle school and said, "Please sir, can I have some more" in your little British accent so perfectly.

Or when you were the spotlight operator for *The Boys Next Door* in high school, and I was stage managing, and you were thirty minutes late for your call and didn't give a shit, and we got into an enormous fight over the headset.

Or the time you made me go see the String Cheese Incident at Radio City Music Hall, and I threw my back out on the way to the concert walking down the stairs of my apartment building on Third Avenue and Twenty-Eighth Street but went to the concert anyway because I knew how much it meant to you. Our seats were in the balcony and every time people jumped around, which happened excessively, the balcony would shake and I was certain we would die in a balcony-collapse freak accident.

Or the time we saw Phish at Coney Island and it was outdoors and rained the entire night, and I was wearing a white dress that was soaked all the way through and shivering on the train the whole two-hour ride back to Queens.

I remember that you used to suck your third and fourth fingers relentlessly so that they had these permanent indentations on them and you would drag your little, white blanket behind you everywhere you went, like Linus. The only time it wasn't in your possession is when you had it in the freezer. You liked it best when it was really cold.

I remember the day you got the *Freaks and Geeks* box set. I got home around four in the afternoon and sat down next to you for what was supposed to be a momentary hello, but I was still sitting in the same spot at four in the morning. It's filed away as one of my all-time favorite memories—just sitting with my brother, watching TV for twelve hours straight.

I remember that time when you were three or four years old, and you ran through Luby's Cafeteria during dinner rush screaming "*Shit, shit, shit!*" and Mom warned you that she was going to wash your mouth out with soap, but you kept doing it. When we got home, she felt it was important to follow through but didn't have bar soap, so she just squirted a bunch of liquid soap into your mouth. Before the soap could foam up and do its job, she immediately felt guilty and started scraping out the inside of your mouth with a washcloth. You were hysterical. She was hysterical. She spent the rest of the night apologizing, crying, and rocking you back and forth in the living room.

I didn't remember this particular exchange from 2011 but got chills after I found it while digging through my Gmail archives for Aziz's *New York Times* piece.

> **Me:** harris i had the most awful dream about you
> it was the saddest dream i've ever had

**Harris:** oh no!

hurry cause i'm goin back to bed

**Me:** you died

and i was grieving

and my life was destroyed

the end

don't die

goodnite

# 27

—

## Before

### Early December 2014

My parents left LA the Sunday after Thanksgiving with a promise from Harris that he would come home after the *Parks and Rec* wrap party in early December, which was being held in Vegas. *Where he'd relapsed a month before.* Of course, after the wrap party, Harris had to turn in a script for *Master of None*, so the trip was further delayed. Then he had some Emerson College master-class to teach. He was scheduled to come home on the second, then the ninth, then the eleventh. He finally got on a plane and made it home Sunday, December 14.

That night, I read *Baby Beluga* three times and *Pat the Bunny* four times. I rocked the baby and smelled her head and laid her gently in her crib. I kissed my husband goodbye and drove the fifteen minutes to my parents' building, sick with anxiety and anticipation. In the elevator. Up seventeen floors. Down the hall. Into the apartment. Dad was watching TV on the living room couch. He barely acknowledged me.

Inside the guest room, all the lights were off, but light from the hallway spilled into the room to reveal a miserable, sick, empty version of my brother curled up feebly on the bed. He moaned and writhed in pain. His body temperature was up and down and up and down. There was sweating, shivering, aches and pains, nausea and occasional vomiting. It felt like I was watching *The Basketball Diaries,* which I found difficult to watch when it was just Leonardo DiCaprio playing a role. My little brother was in agonizing pain, and there was nothing I could do to help him. It was the worst thing I'd ever seen, worse than I ever imagined. *This* was what detox looked like.

Fuck you, heroin. Fuck you.

I sat on the edge of the bed, holding Harris's hand, trying not to audibly sob. My worst nightmare was that I would lose him, and it now felt closer than ever. We didn't say much, maybe even nothing. I mostly sat there and shared the space with him. All the anger faded away. My brother wasn't a selfish asshole who was determined to ruin my life. In fact, this wasn't about me at all. My brother was sick. *Sick.* And all I wanted in this moment was to be there for him.

On the way home, I called a friend who had gotten sober years before and had managed to stay sober, get married, and have a couple of kids. He was confident that the only chance Harris had for success was long-term care. Ninety days was okay; 120 was ideal. Thirty days was akin to doing nothing at all. Thirty days produced just another high: the high of sobriety. You feel great after thirty days, better than you'd ever felt before, and in this euphoric state, you think, I can use *just one more time.* Harris had no chance of kicking this thing if he continued to do thirty-day stints. He'd already failed twice. Something in his approach had to change. My friend gave me the names of several excellent facilities in the Texas area. I wrote them all down and thanked him profusely. I would have to have a conversation with Harris tomorrow—a real conversation, no bullshit, no eggshells.

Unfortunately, it's hard to have a conversation with someone who is in a coma, unresponsive. Talking to Harris felt a lot like that. I headed to my mom's after work the following day. It was around four thirty in the afternoon. The shades were drawn in the living room. I sat on a stool at the kitchen island, eating cheese, while Harris laid on the couch a few feet away. It was hard for him to sit up for more than a few minutes at a time. My mom and I urged him to check into a local detox facility, to do this under medical supervision. It was too much to do on his own and medically unsafe. Seeing the state he was in, I tried not to bombard him with too much but ended up saying most of the stuff that'd been piling up for months. I told him he was going to die if he kept living like this. I told him I wanted him to be there to see his niece go to kindergarten, graduate from college, walk down the aisle. I told him about the necessity of long-term care—he had to give it time. He had to relearn how to function without drugs, and history had proven the futility of thirty days.

He said very little but was open to moving into a sober living facility once he got back to LA. He also agreed to go to a hospital here in Houston to finish detoxing safely, under medical supervision. Thank God. It would be a short stay, a few days at most, but it was something.

He checked himself in, and as soon as he'd gotten the heroin out of his system, he checked himself out. We didn't even have time to visit—it was that quick. Harris had no desire to stay in some rehab on the outskirts of Houston. If the first rehab was the Ritz and the second was the Holiday Inn, this was a Motel 6 on the side of a dirt road next to a state prison. He was still extremely lifeless and depleted once the drugs were out of his system, which continued to take a toll on his body, but he was no longer having the severe physical symptoms I saw a few days earlier that had scared me so much.

However, since sobriety/relapse was now a pattern, I suspected the urge to use was still very much alive.

## 28

—

## Before

December 22, 2014

My mom's birthday fell two days after Harris checked out of the local detox facility. It was also three days before Christmas. She had made reservations months ago at her favorite steak house in Houston and made sure about twenty-five times via email, voicemail, and group text that Harris would be home for the occasion. I'd arranged for a babysitter. But nothing was as we thought it would be and no one felt like steak, so she canceled the reservation. Knowing how disappointed she was about everything, I threw together an extremely last-minute pizza party at our house.

It was clear that my mom needed a formal opportunity to make a wish, so I bought her a giant, white sheet cake with white icing from the grocery store bakery and some colorful birthday candles. These shitty white cakes have always been her favorite. Harris obviously wasn't in the mood to celebrate or even sit up, for that matter. He wanted to stay home in the dark, but she begged and guilted and nagged and pleaded, if only to come to my house for a little while, to which he begrudgingly agreed but showed up an hour late and had a hard time doing anything other than lying on the couch or smoking alone on the back porch. I joined him outside after dinner, of which Harris couldn't eat a single bite. Star Pizza was always his favorite, but he was still too sick to keep anything down.

There, on the porch, it was finally just the two of us. No Iris, no Mike, no Mom, no Dad, no texting or computer screens, no 1,500 miles. Just us. Just me and my little brother having a face-to-face conversation in real time. It was the last just-us, face-to-face conversation in real time we'd ever have.

I pushed the screen door open, and it slammed loudly behind me. The night smelled refreshingly wintery for Texas. Harris was sitting on a brown wicker armchair with festive Hawaiian-print seat cushions, holding a lit cigarette in his left hand and texting with his right. I sat down on the matching love seat across from him and smiled. A peace offering, if you will. He put the phone down in his lap and placed his deflated attention on me.

"You feeling okay?" I knew the answer but had to start somewhere.
He shrugged.

We sat there for a few moments in silence. I watched him smoke. I had smoked a pack a day for over ten years and quit cold turkey seven years earlier. I'd long ago lost the urge to smoke, but all I wanted in this moment was to chain-smoke a dozen cigarettes in a row. I remember how we used to climb out on the roof at our old house on Dumfries to smoke cigarettes after our parents went to bed. I disabled the alarm system on my bedroom window so that it wouldn't beep when the window opened. One day when I was fifteen or sixteen, my dad brought home an ashtray, presented it to me, and said, "If you're going to kill yourself by smoking, please do it outside. I don't want to rush you to emergency room at three in the morning because you've fallen off the roof."

"Do you think therapy is helping?" I asked Harris.

"I don't know. He keeps trying to uncover something awful that happened in my childhood that fucked me up, but it was all so normal, right? I mean, you and Ben gave me a whip-it when I was eleven, but—"

"So this my fault?"

"No."

The scene he's referring to flashed in my mind. Me, Harris, and Ben all sitting on the floor of my bedroom doing whip-its with a metal cracker and balloon, sucking in the nitrous oxide, holding our breaths, and falling backward for thirty seconds at a time. Harris was wearing his Little League uniform.

"'Cause I was fourteen. I was a kid too."

"I know, but you didn't turn into a drug addict," he said.

"And?"

"I mean, I resent it."

"You resent that I'm not a drug addict?"

"Just bein' honest. I'm supposed to be honest now."

"Okay. Well, for the record, I don't take responsibility for you shooting heroin." A tense silence fell between us. "Do you really think I did this to you?"

"No." Pause. "Dad did."

"What?" I ask incredulously. "What does that even mean?"

"I don't know. I can't love. Like Dad. I literally don't know how to connect to people with my emotions."

"Harris, at some point you're gonna have to take responsibility for your own shit."

"I know. I know it's no one's fault. I'm the fuck-up. These are just feelings."

"You're not a fuck-up! You're everyone's favorite! How do you not know that? People love you—we all love you—but you disconnect. *You* do that. You disconnect from me all the time."

"Steph, that's not true! I love Iris and Mike, but you got married and had a baby and that was kind of it for us."

"So I abandoned you?"

"That's not what I meant. We just stopped being best buds—or at least that's how it felt."

The door opened and my mom walked out holding the baby who needed to eat.

And the conversation was over.

# 29

## Ten Months, Three Days

If I were Mom, I can't imagine wanting to celebrate another birthday ever again now that you're gone. I certainly don't. And yet her birthday comes again this year the same as it has every other year. Six of her friends put together a small birthday lunch in honor of her sixty-fifth birthday and ask me to join them. I pick Mom up around noon and we ride over to the restaurant together. In the car, we talk about you. We always—and only—talk about you. Or Iris. We talk about her, too.

Once seated, everyone pours a glass of prosecco and makes a toast to beautiful Maureen. They say all sorts of loving, supportive things, which she deserves a thousand times over.

I am last to speak. I raise my glass high, say "Fuck this year," and pour it down my throat.

A decade ago, things were good. You were alive in body and spirit. You were the real Harris, the one before the drugs. We made that elaborate birthday video for Mom on her fifty-fourth birthday that she loved. Remember that video? We drove around Houston all day, smoking cigarettes and shooting hours of footage, which you edited—expertly, in my opinion. We seem so happy in it. I watched it several times in a row after Mom's birthday luncheon. I love how it starts. You used the first section of that Bright Eyes song about the woman who's flying to meet her fiancé and the plane crashes, and as it's going down, the stranger beside her pretends to throw her a birthday party, and he says, "Happy birthday, darling. We love you very, very, very, very, very, very, very much."

We loved that part. Even though it's about a bunch of people plunging to their deaths, there's still something so uplifting about it. You used it to underscore the intro title card, which read: *"Happy Birthday, Mama. Your family loves you very, very, very much... So, here you go."*

The first shot fades up on you at our first location. You're sitting at a table, a textured wall behind you, distracted by the goings-on of the noisy restaurant. "So basically," you say, "before we started shooting this video, we thought, let's get into the mind of Mom. You know, let's delve into the depths of—"

The camera pans up to a bouncy, boyish waiter at our favorite Vietnamese restaurant, the go-to when the bars close at 2:00 a.m.

"What's up, how you doin'?" he asks.

Focusing the camera on the waiter, I ask him to say happy birthday into the camera: "Happy birthday to me!"

I laugh. He bounces around a little bit more.

"To who?" he asks.

"To Mommy," I reply.

Exuberantly, he shouts "To Mommy! Happy birthday, Mommy!"

I pan back to you. You're laughing and genuinely enjoying the spirited exchange.

"I'm gonna put some fish sauce here," the waiter says. "Use it for your fried egg rolls. Here are some tofu spring rolls." He turns to the camera as if he's addressing Mom and says: "It's what your daughter likes." (He knows this because I used to come in there no less than four or five times a week for these spring rolls. God, they're so good. I want them right now.)

"My mom likes these, too," I tell him.

"She likes that, too? Okay!" And he darts away.

I pan back over to you, giving me a thumbs-up. "Okay, carry on, young Harris."

You raise your eyebrows and smile. "As I was saying, we decided to come to Mai's because, you know, Mom loves the spring rolls. We figured this was a good place to start our venture into the world of Mother. And also, um, thank you for lunch, Mom. We are charging it to the credit card."

The next shot is you swiping the credit card at the checkout counter. "Thanks, Mom."

*Title card: We then wanted to speak with all the people who come into contact with Mom on a regular basis. As it turns out, all of them are Vietnamese.*

Next, we interview the lady who used to do all of Mom's tailoring and several women who work at her nail salon. One of them says, "Happy birthday, Maureen. We love you all here!"

*Title card: Isn't that sweet? They love you all here. Every single one of you.*

Later that night, we interview your drunk friends. All of them are sitting around a green-felt card table in the extra room of our old house that was haunted and always ten degrees colder than the rest of the house. Remember when Mom held a séance with that woman named Madame Buttons the summer we moved in to exorcise the bad energy? So fucking weird.

We tore down the house that used to sit on our property and built a new one when I was in the third grade. A Jewish family of four had lived there before us. We knew them peripherally. They belonged to the Jewish Community Center and went to the same neighborhood schools. They looked like us: a mother, a father, a son, a daughter. They seemed so normal. But the husband snapped one day and pulled a knife on his wife in the kitchen. His son was in the house. The mother screamed at him to run and get help, but by the time he got back, it was too late. His father had killed his wife and then killed himself. And their kids were left without parents. They were the token tragic story everyone talked about. I wonder if this is how people feel about us now. Are we the token tragic story everyone talks about now?

The craziest part is that a few years ago, you randomly ran into the daughter (who is now a grown-up) in an LA comedy club, and she recognized you because you said the name of our street growing up in your act: Dumfries. And that was the name of her street. That was the name of her street where she lived when her father killed her mother then killed himself. That was where she lived when her entire world changed in a single moment.

Anyway, the room upstairs is haunted, and you and your friends used to play poker up there. In the video, there are ten of you hanging out, drinking beer, and playing cards. It's extremely loud. That room was always extra echoey: "Hi, Maureeeen!" They all chime in and latch on to the end of her name and scream it out and raise their beers and make toasts.

*Title card: What they meant to say was they love you...and thank you for letting them constantly destroy your home.*

*Now let us here from the man*—you spelled *hear* like *here*; if you were alive, I would text you now and give you all sorts of shit about it—who we all love… *but seriously wonder how on earth he ever became a doctor.*

Cut to Dad, standing in the middle of your room wearing cargo shorts and a dirty, white T-shirt: "Say, um, Maureen Morris Wittels, you think I miss you or is this a banana in my pocket?" He laughs heartily at his own joke, takes the banana out of his pocket, and starts to peel it. He sits down on the foot of your bed and continues: "Fifty-four years old. (*Sigh.*) Not a kid anymore but more beautiful than ever. And, um, happy birthday. Sorry your life hasn't worked out like you planned it, but hey, it's your own fault, you married me, but I digress, so um…" He takes a bite then rubs the banana all over his nose. "So, um, happy birthday." He sticks it in his ear. "Hey is this a banana in my ear? And, I love you. Bye Bye."

*Title: And now, what the kids have to say…*

Cut to you, sitting in a spinning desk chair in front of a backdrop of red curtains that hung in your room growing up. You say, "Um, my stand-up career actually got started by trying to make Mom laugh. The old toothbrush-up-the-ass-draw-a-smiley-face-on-your-ass trick—uh, that's still one of my most popular bits that I do today on stage."

Then you cut to a close-up of my face in my room doing this stupid nasally voice that always made Mom laugh. It's really stupid and grating. I have no idea why she liked it. "Hi, Mom, this is my birthday message to you. I just wanted to say happy birthday and I love you very, very, very much, and it's really nice of you when you gave me a bath when I had to get my mucus sucked out of my face because I was dirty and for a mommy to do that to her big child is so nice, and you're the nicest mommy ever in the whole wide world, and I love you and, um, I just want to say happy birthday."

Then, back to you: "Mom always had unorthodox parenting techniques. Brings me back to the time I had a wart on my hand and mom swore the trick was a raw potato. Can't be cooked, can't be french-fried, lyonnaise, can't be anything. It has to be raw. She cut it in half, made me rub it on the wart, and then buried it in the backyard. I think it had to be like a full moon or something. And I thought it was very weird. But the wart did in fact go away. Granted, it went away after I went to a real 'doctor' [air quotes] and he 'froze it off' [air quotes] 'medically' [air quotes]. But I still hold the potato largely responsible for that wart being gone today." You do your little pinched-lip, Harris nod. An early version of your original Small Mouth character. "Happy birthday, Mom, love you." Then, you purse your lips into the shape of a kiss and follow it up with an awkward grin and eyebrow raise.

The music swells: "Birthday" by the Beatles.

*Title Card: Happy Birthday! We Love You!*

# 30

—

## Before

### December 25, 2014

Every family has its traditions. Even though we grew up in a Jewish household, Christmas was ours. It doesn't make any sense, but the root of it is that my dad didn't want us to feel left out, so he incorporated Santa Claus into our childhood and, over time, it grew and grew into this epic family tradition. As kids, we would leave milk and cookies out for Santa and the reindeers and spend long, restless nights in sleepless anticipation of all the epic shit awaiting our frenzied entrance. We would wake up before the sun came up and run into a living room littered with perfectly wrapped presents. Presents on the floor, presents on the table, presents on the sofa, presents in the kitchen. Wrapped presents, presents in gift bags, presents in envelopes. Presents everywhere. Only crumbs remained on the plate we'd left out and the milk was all gone. A letter from Santa sat on the fireplace underneath the Christmas stockings that were stuffed with lottery tickets, candy, and *Playboy* magazines for Harris, compliments of my dad, the resident weirdo. Over the years, the letters became the focal point of the day. It was the one time a year when "Santa" expressed his feelings to the "little girl" and "little boy" who lived in our house. It meant a lot to all of us.

Naturally, Iris's first Christmas was a big deal, and I wanted it to be special for her despite all the heavy shit that was weighing the rest of us down. I was still bothered by what Harris said on the porch but had chosen to go with the reasonable side of my brain that assured me he didn't mean it. I just wanted him to stay sober, and making it about my poor, hurt feelings wasn't a means to that end. Love was the best thing I could offer at this point. And what better day to give it than on Christmas?

We got to my parents' around 10:00 a.m. to find the room littered with presents, all for Iris. Presents on the floor, presents on the table, presents on the sofa, presents in the kitchen. Wrapped presents, presents in gift bags, presents in envelopes. Presents everywhere. We tried to do the whole happy Christmas morning song and dance for her benefit, but it was hard to muster the strength. Especially for Harris. He tried to participate but was still so sick from detox and had to go back to bed within minutes.

After Iris opened the last of her presents and scraps of wrapping paper coated the floor of the living room, I found a check for $6,000 sitting on the kitchen counter, folded up in a piece of scrap paper from a Houston SPCA notepad. On the bottom of the page sat a picture of a dog and cat playing with a blue ball of yarn. Scribbled in pencil on the back of the paper was a note that read:

> *Sorry for no card.*
> *I've been going through stuff if you haven't noticed.*
> *Anyways.*
> *Here is to being besties again.*
> *Hope this helps with Iris in some way.*
> *Love you*
> *—Brother*

Only a couple days earlier I'd been complaining about the burden of Iris's hearing aids not being covered by insurance and having to pay up to $6,000 out of pocket when her loaner pair expires. My stress was apparent. Even with all the shit he'd been going through, Harris still managed to hear me. He still managed to come through and save the day. I was so grateful. I couldn't do these sorts of things for him. We got him a gift card to Chili's. I mean, he loved Chili's, but it was no $6,000.

## 31

## Ten Months, Five Days

It's our first Christmas without you.

How did we get from *there* to *here*? Last Christmas Eve, you were home. You were alive. You were detoxing. It was agony, but you were here.

The Christmas Eve before, I was eight months pregnant. A world of promise curled up inside my belly. Mike brought home a key lime pie, my favorite. We ate it together on the sofa, right out of the box with two forks.

The Christmas Eve before that, Mike proposed to me in bed in the middle of the night, one year to the minute after we'd met. It was as joyous a moment as I've known.

Ten years ago, our family was making s'mores by the fireplace in our childhood home. We stuck marshmallows on unfurled wire coat hangers. We let them catch fire. Our overweight cocker spaniel, Buster, kept stealing them off the table as they cooled.

This Christmas Eve, you are dead. Permanently and forever gone.

Once it gets dark, we drive around and look at Christmas lights, as we do every year. Iris, Mom, and Dad are in the back seat. Mike drives. I sit in the passenger seat. Iris is on the hunt for Santa Claus, or "Kiki Cause," as she calls him. She keeps shouting, "Bapa! Where Kiki Cause?!" Dad tells her to keep her eyes peeled. He said the same thing to us when we were little.

We drive slowly around the mansion-clad neighborhood of River Oaks with the windows rolled down, since it's eighty degrees in Houston. We see sprawling trees dripping with twinkling lights, inflatable Santas and snowmen, and nativity scenes. We sing "Jingle Bells" and "Rudolph, the Red Nosed Reindeer."

At some point, Dad quietly says, "We used to drive over here every Christmas Eve to look at these lights." The car goes silent. And the silence says what it always says: *Harris should be here.* It's the same sound the fireworks made on our first Fourth of July without you. As we watched the epic fireworks show from Mom and Dad's balcony, Mom grabbed me by the waist and held on tight. Every exploding mass of light whispered *Harris*, and we both heard it.

There's no way to tune it out. It's a frequency that's always ringing in our ears.

Christmas Day is even worse. It knocks me down, drags me out by my hair, and leaves me dismembered all over again.

Iris wakes up at 5:55 a.m., but I've been awake for the last half hour, lying in bed, thinking about Christmas mornings when we were kids. I remember getting one of those little red and yellow Cozy Coupe cars one year and you and I taking turns riding it up and down our block. When I was six, we got our cocker spaniel. You wanted to name him *Ghostbuster*. I threw a fit, so Dad used it as an opportunity to teach us about compromise: we settled on *Buster*. He lived until he was sixteen. I was a junior in college. His death was really hard on you. We loved that dog.

I turn off the baby monitor, throw on my robe, and walk down the hall to Iris's room. I lift her out of her crib, and she wraps her little arms tightly around my neck. It's the best part of my day. We sit in the big rocking chair where she lays on my lap with her head nestled against my chest. We rock back and forth as she slowly wakes up. After a few quiet moments, she pops up, looks at me, and starts giggling. I giggle back. She giggles back. This goes on for several rounds.

"Light," she says and points to the lamp. I turn it on. Our eyes squint to adjust.

"Iris, guess who you're gonna see today?"

"*Ummm...*"

"Santa Claus!"

"He 'cary."

"No, he's not scary. He is a nice man who brings presents to good little boys and girls. Are you a good girl?"

"Yeah!"

"Well, Santa came to Momo-Bapa's house last night and brought lots of presents for Iris. Do you want some presents?"

"*Yeah!* I open dem!"

"That's right. How many presents will you open?"

"*Ummm*, tree!"

"Three? How about ten?"

"Yeah, ten!"

Iris is electrified. She jumps out of my lap, and the whirlwind of our morning routine begins. I soundcheck and put in her hearing aids, she demands milk, we migrate downstairs, she eats grapes—lots of grapes—and watches episodes of *Daniel Tiger's Neighborhood*, *Angelina Ballerina*, and *Barney*. Mike heads downstairs around 8:00 a.m. in his colorful Peruvian robe; I purchased one for each of us on our second anniversary, the cotton year. They're from the Hotel Havana where we stayed in San Antonio during our road trip through West Texas last December.

We take turns getting dressed. Between Iris having a meltdown when I leave the room to take a shower and Mike locking himself in his office to handwrite his eight-page letter from Santa, we are running a solid hour behind. Mom texts me several times that morning about bagels and lox, eggs and biscuits, and a list of grocery stores that would be open on Christmas Day. It's the most Jewish correspondence a person could ever have on Christmas morning.

We finally arrive at their house a little after 10:00 a.m. As we pull up to the building, Iris starts clapping and screaming, *"Momobapa!"* She often combines their names into one name. We get out of the car, and Iris runs to the elevators to press the Up button. We ride up seventeen floors. She jumps up and down. She always loves to jump up and down in a moving elevator. When the doors open, she and the dog chase each other down the long hallway to their door. Dad opens it with an enthusiasm strictly reserved for Iris. I catch a glimpse into the living room, littered with presents. More presents than any almost-two-year-old would ever need or deserve. But this isn't really for her. It's for them. They need this the most.

She doesn't know where to start. She bangs on a big box and starts tearing the paper off it in tiny pieces. She lights up when a remote-controlled Olaf appears. She is excited to hear him say, "Hi! I'm Olaf, and I like warm hugs" when she presses the little button on his hand. A noise-making toy is such a dick move. He holds her attention for about twenty-five seconds until she moves on to the next shiny object, rips the paper off, throws it all over the room, plays with the thing inside for several seconds, gets distracted by the next shiny object, etc. She's having a ball.

But the focal point of Christmas Day has never been the presents. It's always been the annual letter from "Santa." Sometimes I would read it; sometimes you would. But Dad was always the one to watch. He wore the most content and satisfied look on his face as they were read. Dad never excelled at expressing his emotions, but this was his way. This was how he told us how proud he was of us, how much joy we brought him, how much he loved us.

All the letters now sit in an orange file folder labeled *Santa Letters* in a file cabinet in my guest-bedroom closet. Collectively, they read like a Wittels family history. The oldest letter dates back to 1985, when I was four and you were one. Up until 1999, they were all composed in Dad's illegible chicken scratch. Post-2000, Santa got a PC and started typing the letters.

Dad's notes to you feel especially poignant in hindsight. Reading through them now feels like an exercise in Greek tragedy. I want to cry out to the protagonist, *"Hey! You're doomed! Pay attention! Take another path!"* But that's the thing about Greek tragedy: the hero's downfall is inevitable. That's why it's so tragic. The audience feels pathos because they know what's coming but can't do anything to stop it.

Here are some of my favorite excerpts from Santa's notes to you:

2000

*When you were small, your parents could protect you from most trouble and problems. As you get older, your parents cannot protect you from many troubles and problems. Santa has confident that your mother's teachings will help you to make the right decisions when things don't go your way.*

*Thank you for the milk and cookies. Santa is a hungry dude.*

*Love*

S. CLAUS

*The Clauses*

2007

*HARRIS—A REGULAR DYNAMO IN LA. HARRIS, TOO MUCH WORRY IS NOT GOOD FOR A COMEDIAN OR ANYONE ELSE, TAKES A LOT OF TIME AND WORK TO LEARN AN ACT. CHIMNEY SLIDING WAS HARD FOR SANTA TO LEARN. LAST HARD THING I REMEMBER. HAVE FUN AND PLEASE TELL YUR FATHER ALL ABOUT THE FUN. THE OLD GUY NEEDS A THRILL. HAVE FUN, ENJOY, LAUGH, LOVE, AND USE PROTECTION.*

2009

*Harris, thank goodness you got your dada's hair and body. U never looked better. Truly LA and getting famous. U do know how to live. The number of people u know and things u have accomplished are incredible. Santa has not met his next door neighbors and has trouble accomplishing a BM.*

*But prepare for leaner days. The only thing that never goes down is old mrs claus. But that is for a different letter.*

## 2010

*Harris—if you work hard, your mother worries that you are too tired and that you will burn out. If you are not working hard, your mother worries that your career is over. Either way she gets to worry and she does enjoy a good worry. Your father worries that he will not get to see pictures of your dates.*

*It is good to take time to relax, recharge batteries. It is not only what you do, but the kind of person you are. Do not work so hard that you lose yourself, because yourself is terrific and to lose it would be a real lose. Besides there is no sense working for the money, the new communist governor of California will take all your money. Remember that it is raining in LA, so do not forget to wear your rubbers. The claus' are really proud of you.*

## 2011

*Harris, the old demented frail santa and the hot, sexy, voluptuous mrs claus are sooo proud of you. U have accomplished so much in so short a time. U have so much going on and have had so much success in all that you have done. Mrs claus is always able to find the dark lining in every silver cloud and worries that you have too much going on. Save some energy for you. You are gifted and talented and very cool and you are also beautiful. Clearly you both have inherited your father's good looks. Harris, the only person who can stop you from reaching your goals is you.*

2014

*Dear people;*

*This year almost did Santa in. 2014 had unbelievable ups and downs. Talking of ups and downs, there are always the insatiable needs of Mrs. Claus. Old Santa is worn down. It wasn't that there was good and there was bad, it was the rapid changes from good to bad and back. Let us remember:*

*Stephanie had a little girl BUT, The little girl has a hearing problem.*

*We were told and thought that this precious baby could have the worst genetic hearing problem possible. BUT lots of tests later, No she did not have a bad genetic problem. Now, you are told that she has a mild, moderate, severe hearing loss—Whatever that means. The baby is a normal, really smart 11 month old.*

*Iris even gets up in a great mood BUT she gets up at 5 a.m.*

*The voluptuous Mrs. Claus gives new meaning to "thar she blows" Sorry, Santa also has fantasies that will never happen*

*Mike has finished 1 full year of selling real estate, but Mike had some slow times*

*Mike sold lots of real estate recently—he is establishing himself and doing it fast*

*Hold on. Stop the letter. What, not now Mrs. Claus I am busy. Start without me. Insatiable I tell you.*

*Mike is taking his wife and daughter to Phoenix BUT, Mike is driving his wife and daughter to Phoenix. Can you all join Santa in saying "That is really a fucked idea." Stephanie believes in Mike. Wonderful to see. Let us see if she still believes in him after she reaches Phoenix.*

*Harris knows lots of people in LA and does lots of great things.*

*Harris still loves writing, but Harris has had some rough times. Harris is working hard at doing better. It is tough.*

*We love and support Harris. He is worth it.*

*Stephanie, Mike and Harris—wonderful people BUT there are lost liberals. We pray that they find in their brains what scientists call the O'Reilly factor.*

*Iris is the spirit in the family. Mrs. Claus holds the family together. Santa peas a lot.*

*Santa thinks this is the most wonderful Christmas of all. This year we were all tested and we survived as individuals and as a family. Say what you want, think what you want, one thing is clear—We have been here for one another this very tough year.*

*So, keep the faith. Trust 2015 will be lots better and Santa will see you next year.*

That was the last letter Santa ever wrote. I read it aloud last December as you lay on the couch, shivering, wrapped up in a hoodie and a blanket, watching your niece eat wrapping paper off the floor.

Now that you're gone, Dad is done writing letters. Now that you're gone, Dad is just done. So this year, Mike takes over.

Iris gets her first letter from Santa this Christmas morning. It's eight pages handwritten and sits on the coffee table in a bulging, fat envelope labeled *Iris* in red crayon. I pick up the letter as Iris opens her last present and start to read it aloud.

Mom quickly interrupts. "Let's finish with these gifts first." I put the letter in my lap until Iris finishes, then try to start again, but Mom is busying herself with the toy manual to the battery-operated Olaf. She refuses to look at Mike or me. She doesn't want to pay attention, and it's really fucking annoying to me. "Mom, Mike worked on this for five hours."

She puts down the card and focuses her attention on Mike.

I continue reading and do fine until I get to this paragraph:

"This year has been hard. Uncle Harris left way too soon. It's like a big crater was left in Mommy, Momo, Bapa, and Daddy. It's hard to explain to you now, but any time they thought it was too much, they'd see your smile, hear your laugh, or remember something hilarious you did, you'd start building more and more ground around that crater. Everyone loves you so much for that. I'm sure Uncle Harris is thankful that you're able to make them smile."

I pause. I breathe. I try to keep reading, but when I get to the next part about Mom working to help other families with craters, I throw my head down and audibly weep. Mom cries, too. Dad has tears in his eyes.

"These are supposed to be funny," I say.

"Not much to be funny about this year," Dad replies.

Iris continues to play with Olaf.

## 32

---

## Before

### December 26, 2014

The day after her first Christmas, eleven-month-old Iris, Mike, and I packed up the Ford Explorer and drove far, far away from Houston and my parents and Harris and heroin. The destination was Phoenix, and we got there via West Texas. It was a lovely road trip for the most part, except for the eleven-hour stretch between Marfa and Phoenix, where I developed a head cold and Iris was done with her car seat thirty minutes in, and I wanted us to drive the car right off the road but played hours of *Yo Gabba Gabba!* on the iPad instead. It mostly worked.

I hated to leave Harris in the state he was in and wouldn't had I known it would be the last time I saw him, but the plan was for him to check into a rehab in LA and move into sober living. Nobody, including Harris, trusted that he could get from our parents' house in Houston to a rehab in LA without relapsing, so my mom flew out there with him to act as bodyguard. She didn't let him out of her sight, except for one night when he begged her to let him go visit his friends Paul and Lesley for an hour, just to talk and reconnect. He swore it would be fine and that she could trust him.

Once she got him checked in, she headed back to Houston

feeling relieved and a little more at ease. Third time's a charm. Or three strikes, you're out. No one was sure which it would be, but we crossed our fingers and hoped for the best. It was hard to stay hopeful after two relapses, but we wanted him to get better and hope was really our only option. If we were godly people, I guess we would have prayed. But we weren't. So, we hoped. We mostly hoped he could start to love himself because that was the only way any of this would stick.

When my mom checked him in, they put him in the detox facility instead of the sober living facility, which didn't make any sense. He'd already gone through detox when he was home in Houston. I saw it. He was sick, and he detoxed. He'd been sober for two weeks now. Why another detox?

It's so clear in hindsight. He relapsed while my mom was staying at his house. Going through his texts, months and months after he died, in the middle of the night while lying next to my sleeping husband, I found a text he sent to a friend at one in the morning the night before he checked in: I had two clean weeks and just relapsed because I wanted a last hurrah and now I'm like why the fuck did I do that.

He put in all that hard work for nothing. We had all those conversations for nothing. My mom flew all the way out there to make sure he was safe, and he used anyway. What a shitty, fucked-up, selfish thing to do.

His friend replied: Don't beat yourself up, pal, relapse is part of it, but you're playing with fire. Harris asked her not to tell his ex-girlfriend, the one who contacted me in November over Facebook to tell me about the relapse at the Phish show: She will tell my family and then they will no longer speak to me. Then she told him to get out of LA. We said the same thing. That's all we wanted.

Would it have made a difference?

# 33

## Ten Months, One Week

Back in July, Mom and I anticipated that our first Christmas without you would destroy us—again—so we booked an Expedia trip to some gigantic resort in Playa del Carmen with a pirate themed-water park for kids and all-inclusive alcohol for parents. The idea was to put distance between us and your absence, but you only come into greater focus on our first family vacation without you.

We all fly to Mexico the day after Christmas. The most magical part of the trip is the moment Iris sees the ocean for the first time. It will forever be cemented into my memory as one of those glorious life moments that makes you feel lucky to be alive. I haven't felt much of those lately, so I treasure this one. First, she feels the sand between her toes and giggles. She keeps digging them deeper and deeper into the earth. When she looks up from her feet and spots the ocean, her eyes light up and her jaw drops open and she looks at me as if to say, *"Mama, can you believe this!?"* She runs right toward it without hesitation. As soon as her toes touch the water, she rips off her shirt and pants and stands there in a diaper, in the ocean. She laughs and laughs and laughs. An expression of sheer joy.

I think, *God, why are you not here to see this?*

Iris is about the same age as you were in that home movie from 1986, where you, me, Mom, and Dad are all standing together on an overcast beach in Galveston, Texas. You're wearing a bright yellow shirt and blue-and-white-striped overalls with a red fire truck on the front. The wind is fierce, so Mom and Dad have to keep shouting back and forth at each other, narrating the scene for the camera.

"Are you filming us?" Mom asks.

"Who are you?" Dad jokes.

"Oh, we are your wife and two children. We're in Galveston."

He focuses the camera on me. "What's your name, little girl?"

"Stephanie!" I shout.

He focuses the camera on you. "What's your name, little boy?"

"Tell him, Harris," Mom urges.

But you keep wandering away from the camera, so distracted by the water. You jump up and down and make splashes that are taller than you are. I follow you as you zig-zag and dance in and out of the water. Mom shouts, "Hey, guys, stay over here!" She reaches both her hands out to pull us closer to her, to keep us safe. This is a mother's instinct.

"Harris, come here," she demands. "Stephanie, out of the water, please!"

Dad says, "Show me the ocean, Harris. Where's the ocean?"

You point to the vast, brown body of water stretched out before you with wonder in your eyes then pick up dead crabs off the wet sand.

With the exception of the lack of free Wi-Fi (which is total bullshit), you would love this place in Mexico. Dining options boil down to several all-you-can-eat buffets—your favorite. There's always an ample amount of boiled shrimp you would have "tore up," as you liked to say. You used to pile your plate high into a food mountain at any buffet, take a few bites, leave the rest, and go back for seconds, thirds, fourths, and fifths. You wanted to try it all. I think you liked the process of getting the food more than you liked eating it. Steamed king crab legs were your top pick, and they had them at all Las Vegas buffets, so Las Vegas buffets were your favorite. You also always went for the mac and cheese, lo mein, egg rolls, crab rangoon, sushi, chicken fingers, fried chicken, mashed potatoes, potatoes au gratin, prime rib, nachos, quesadillas, fried mozzarella sticks, pizza, lasagna, oysters, and any variety of seafood. Never any vegetables or fresh things.

There's this ice cream parlor at the resort that opens every day at 9:00 a.m. and closes at 11:00 p.m. It has a dance floor in the middle that lights up in neon colors wherever you step on it, like that piano at FAO Schwartz. Iris bounces all over the neon floor in only a diaper and a hot pink T-shirt, holding a giant waffle cone in one hand and a spoon in the other. She is a vision. Looking at her dancing in this ice cream parlor, I keep thinking about that podcast you did a while back, where you pretended to call in from heaven:

"Hey, it's Harris, calling from heaven. Uh, it's pretty great up here! It's beautiful, for starters. Uh, Hitler's up here, however, for the vegetarianism thing, so…callin' bullshit on *that*. But other than that, it's pretty great. It is very cloudy, and you, uh, you sit on 'em. That's cool. Ooh, gotta go—ice cream buffet!"

I wonder if there really is a heaven. And I wonder if you're up there, right now, sitting on a cloud, eating ice cream. If so, I hope Phish is playing in the background.

# 34

## Ten Months, One Week, Six Days

Phish was as critical to you as air, water, leftovers, and maybe even heroin. I remember when you got hired on *The Sarah Silverman Program*, and you told her Phish was your religion and that you'd have to continue going to shows even if it conflicted with your work schedule. Every New Year's Eve, you'd take what can only be described as a religious pilgrimage to New York City to see them play at Madison Square Garden. So, at midnight on the last day of the year, I think about how you'd be there now, texting me: Happy New Year, Sister. Love you.

I can't believe we're about to be in the year *after* you died.

On New Year's Day, we visit friends who have twin boys Iris's age. We drink champagne and play Cards Against Humanity while *Thomas the Tank Engine* babysits the kids. George Carlin is in it—did you know that? So random.

On our way home, I sit next to Iris in the back seat. She takes my phone, which she now calls *Iris*. (She thinks the phone is named Iris since the phone contains thousands of photos and videos of her.) She immediately locates the photo app, as any modern baby can do, and scrolls through all the videos. She lands on one of her favorites: you playing guitar.

In it, you're wearing your uniform white T-shirt and jeans and sitting in a spinning office chair. Behind you is a corkboard with lots of thumbtacked, pink index cards. It looks like a writers' room. I assume *Parks*. A woman holding the phone says, "Action." Maybe Aisha? I'm not sure. You smile sheepishly and look down at your fingers as you strum a few intro chords. You sing, "Jumped in the cab, said Jay-Z, yeah I like to play. Feelin kinda homesick, I need a—" and the video cuts off. It was some adorable, acoustic version of Miley Cyrus's "Party in the USA." This is one of Iris's favorite videos. She plays it several times on repeat then looks up at me, smiles, and shouts, "Harris!"

She knows who you are.

I was so worried she wouldn't, but she does. Because you are everywhere. A gigantic painted portrait of you on a wood canvas hangs in our home office. A guy from Instagram painted it and sent us the original portrait out of the kindness of his heart. You're on bookshelves, on walls, and in hallways. You are all over this house.

And she knows who you are.

# 35

---

## Ten Months, Two Weeks, Two Days

Last January was full of hope and promise. You called me on January 4 to check in. You'd only been at rehab number three a few days, but the humanity was already seeping back into your voice. You said this place felt different than the others, and you planned to stay for a good, long while. "There are cool, funny people here who play music. These are my people," you said. All of us were optimistic that *this* would be the time the sober would stick.

Last January was a much-needed fresh start. Things were finally looking up. Iris would turn one that month. We had lived through what we thought was the most turbulent year of our lives—becoming parents of a baby with a disability, spending the first three months of her life in hospitals and doctor's offices, running all sorts of terrifying tests, being told when she was two weeks old that she would grow to struggle academically, socially, and emotionally. But each new sound, new word, new milestone proved this shitty doomsday hypothesis totally wrong.

Our daughter was a force.

My brother was safe and sober and finally in the right place. I knew 2015 would be a good year. The trauma was behind us. And we had survived.

There was so much hope and promise last January.

This January, I wake up feeling like shit. I am neither refreshed nor hopeful. I don't want to go back to work today. I don't want to do anything. I don't want to do anything anymore under these circumstances.

Most days, I wake up to a screaming two-year-old who doesn't understand the distinction between morning and the middle of the goddamn night. Mike and I alternate wake-up days. On my days, I pick her up, smother her in love, rock her back and forth, put in her hearing aids, pour some milk, watch an episode of *Sofia* or *Elmo* or *Mickey Mouse*. I make hash browns, cut grapes, toast mini whole-grain pancakes. She cups her hands over her mouth and says, "Oh my god," or calls her father *Mike* instead of *Daddy*, or attempts to floss her teeth. I think of you whenever she does something funny, which is often.

I mindlessly scroll through Facebook, Instagram, Twitter. I see your friends. I think of you.

I kiss and hug and say *love you* and *have a good day* to Mike and Iris as they head out the door for school, leaving me alone to get myself together. The house is quiet. I think of you.

Sometimes I get back in bed for a few minutes. I think about how I should go to the gym. In some sort of delusional state back in November, I paid for a yearlong membership and have only gone twice. I don't want to go to the gym. I scroll through Facebook, Instagram, Twitter again or answer some emails or pay some bills or do some writing. I make breakfast, usually two eggs and Ezekiel toast. Sometimes, I make a Greek yogurt–fruit-nut bowl thing and think about how you once proclaimed that "all white girls like Greek yogurt."

I shower, stand in my closet, and hate that most of my pants no longer fit. I put something on. I spray some stuff in my hair and scrunch it. I pour my coffee, start the car, turn on a podcast, and drive the eight minutes to work. I turn off the car, linger for a moment, take a deep breath, think of you, and try to prepare myself for the students and the parents and the emails and the lesson plans and the ungraded papers and the letters of recommendation that all wait for me on the other side of the car door. I don't know how to do it anymore. Or maybe I don't want to do it anymore. Or maybe I don't want to do anything anymore. It's hard to tell what's real and what's grief.

The day happens. It takes energy. I mostly want chocolate.

I get back in the car at four o'clock, turn the podcast back on, drive the ten minutes to Iris's school. I think of you.

When I walk through her classroom door, Iris smiles with all of her teeth, which have little spaces in between them like her daddy had when he was her age. She runs hard into my arms. It's a legitimate, daily high. It's a thing I need to keep doing all of these days. We drive home listening to Toddler Tunes on Pandora and calling out all the red lights and green lights along the way. I think this is impressive. I think everything she does is impressive. I think of you.

We pull into the driveway. Iris insists on climbing into the driver's seat. "I drive the car!" She orders me to sit in the back seat. "Seat belt on, Mommy!" This is both adorable and maddening. I watch her press every single button in my car ten times in a row and wait for something to break. I think about how I'll have to drive out to the fucking dealership in the suburbs. Or Mike will do it. Of course, Mike will do it.

He does it all. I think of Mike. I think of what a raw deal he's gotten. *I need to be more present in our marriage,* I think. I must be the world's worst wife. Unpleasant. Detached. Disconnected—emotionally and physically. I try to remember the last time we had sex. It's been so fucking long; I can't. *Please God let him still love me if I ever crawl out of this hole.*

Iris continues to play with the hazard lights. I'm impatient and want a snack and eventually peel her out of the car by bribing her with television.

I cobble together some semblance of dinner—pasta, so much pasta—while she pulls at my shirt and gets out her little metal stepladder to "help" and narrates the TV show and sporadically cries about something the dog did.

We sit down around six. I complain to Mike that I can't eat like this anymore. I long for vegetables but it takes so much work. Iris starts melting down. Depending on the degree of the day's highs and lows, I can sometimes talk her through her feelings calmly and lovingly, assuring her it's okay to be mad and sad. I can offer her hugs and give her pots and pans to bang on as an alternative. Other times, my head falls into my hands or onto the table, I grumble and wait for Mike to intervene. On darker days, I lose my patience and walk away from her completely, leaving her alone and screaming for mommy. I hate myself in these moments. I hate myself in lots of moments.

After dinner, we bathe her, make some jokes, play some hide and seek, put on some pajamas, read *many* books. I think of you. I tell her goodnight, she tells me to go drink apple juice, and Mike puts her to bed.

At this point, I usually collapse into my own bed. Occasionally, I fall asleep. Mostly, Mike and I binge-watch something and tune out the world. I think of you.

I scroll through Facebook, Instagram, Twitter again. I post yet another picture of Iris. I think of you.

Around 11:30, I take 5 mg of Ambien. (Or, lately, 7.5 mg, sometimes 10.) I stole the bottle from your medicine cabinet when we were cleaning out your house. I figured I would need it. I think of you.

The house is quiet. I do some writing. I think of you. I kiss Mike good night and lie there in the dark and eventually fall asleep and wake up too early to the sound of a screaming child. I think of Iris, then I think of you.

It starts all over again. Every day, wading around in the toxic waste of longing for a person who will never return.

I certainly feel moments of intense pride and delight. There are also acute moments of exhaustion and the blood-boiling frustration of constantly negotiating with an individual who has not yet developed the mechanics of rational thought. This is how it is for any parent of a small child. It's all very normal in this way. There are highs and lows. It's just that, in the midst of my highs and lows, I'm always thinking of my dead brother. It adds another layer of low.

Thinking of you is as reflexive as blinking, although the thought is no longer a drone strike. I'm no longer standing in a field, bracing myself, looking up at the sky in terror. This isn't a war zone. This is just how it works now: I feel my feelings of despair, get out of bed, and participate in the world anyway.

I finally understand the meaning of acceptance on the grief chart. It's not that the bereaved ever accepts the death of the loved one—I will never *accept* your death—it's that you come to accept that these really *are* your shitty, irreversible circumstances. One day, it just becomes clear: this is the way it is now. The delusions, denial, hysterics, depression, torment—it eventually starts to melt into this pit of mush that lives in your stomach and just sort of weighs you down. It's not even necessarily fueled by emotion any more. It's just the way your body works now. Like the day you accept that your stomach will never again look the way it did before you grew a child in it. You're never gonna like it, but you'll eventually get to a point where you go to the fucking store and buy pants that are the next size up because you have to wear pants. Acceptance.

January marches on. The mushy-stomach feeling is compounded by the fact that my family has *literally* been sick since early December. I know you hate overuse of the word *literally*, but this is an instance of justified and appropriate usage. On December 21, Iris had to get ear tubes for chronic ear infections, which is a minor surgery with anesthesia and the whole nine. Then, she got another cold and cough a couple days after going back to school. Then Mike got her cold and cough, which developed into bronchitis. I got some horrific cold or flu that forced me into a sleep state for three full days. Two days on the mend and then a sinus infection. Meanwhile, Iris developed pink eye and vomited four times in one night. We literally ran out of clean sheets. The next day, she was running a high fever and had to stay home from school the rest of the week.

Now, we're all stuck watching *Sofia the* (Fucking) *First* on repeat, surrounded by mountains of dirty tissues and coughs that shake the walls of the house. It's hard to be stuck in some sort of emotional feedback loop when four loads of your child's vomit-soaked laundry and pajamas need attention in the middle of the night. In this way, toddlers are an ideal distraction from grief. Everything revolves around them, and everything must be done right now. Trying to get the fever to break, running around the park on a gorgeous day, navigating the world's most irrational tantrum—there's no time to stop and think. It's all go-go-go, now-now-now-now.

I think we're all just doing our best to survive the inevitable pain and suffering that walks alongside us through life. Long ago, it was wild animals and deadly poxes and harsh terrain. I learned about it playing *The Oregon Trail* on an old IBM in my computer class in the fourth grade. The nature of the trail has changed, but we keep trekking along. We trek through the death of a sibling, a child, a parent, a partner, a spouse; the failed marriage, the crippling debt, the necessary abortion, the paralyzing infertility, the permanent disability, the job you can't seem to land; the assault, the robbery, the break-in, the accident, the flood, the fire; the sickness, the anxiety, the depression, the loneliness; the betrayal, the disappointment, and the heartbreak.

There are these moments in life where you change instantly.

In one moment, you're the way you were, and in the next, you're someone else. Like becoming a parent: you're adding, of course, instead of subtracting, as it is when someone dies, and the tone of the occasion is obviously different, but the principle is the same. Birth is an inciting incident, a point of no return, that changes one's circumstances forever. The second that beautiful baby onto whom you have projected all your hopes and dreams comes out of your body, you will never again do anything for yourself. It changes you suddenly and entirely.

Birth and death are the same in that way.

In 2014, there was birth. In 2015, there was death.

And in two years' time, we've experienced both.

I'm no longer the person I was before The Tragedy. I'm becoming someone else. I'm becoming a person I don't yet know.

# 36

—

## A Month Before

### January 2015

We threw Iris her first birthday party the day before her actual birthday. My in-laws flew in and lots of friends attended. It was a celebration-worthy occasion. Iris had made it nearly 365 days in the world, and we had made it nearly 365 days as her parents. Like any significant occasion of late, there was a part of me that was sad that Harris was absent.

The party was at this huge, indoor playland. I knew Iris wouldn't remember any of it, but it was still a success, despite the fact that she refused to take one bite of her cake, much less smush any part of her body in it like babies are supposed to do. She was a notably neat baby and always had been. She never colored on the walls or poured a bag of flour all over the living room. She would find the tiniest pebble of dog food in a corner and bust out her tiny broom and dustpan to rectify the situation. She would wipe up drops of spilled milk with tissues. She loved throwing things in the trash. I worried she might have OCD. Add it to the list.

Harris had sent me an email the day before:

**Subject: my phone dont work here**

i was trying to tell you happy birthday to iris and that i'm
sorry i couldn't be there for it, but i will be next year.

There's priceless footage of Harris's first birthday in my mom's DVD collection. He's sitting in his high chair with shaggy brown hair, wearing a tiny, maroon Oklahoma Sooners shirt—my dad went to University of Oklahoma and is still a die-hard fan.

In the video, my mom puts the whole cake on his tray, and I scream in agony in the background. I want it. Harris pushes his hand into the middle of the cake like he's pulling out a beating heart in that scene from *Indiana Jones: Temple of Doom*. He shoves cake into his mouth by the fistful like a barbarian, coating his entire person in icing.

After a few bites, my mom takes the cake away from Harris and puts it in front of me on the kitchen table. Harris screams and cries. Then she takes the cake away from me and gives it back to Harris. I lose my mind. Mom, Dad, Grandma, Aunt Carol, and Uncle Herb laugh loudly in the background. This goes on for several more rounds. They think it's hilarious.

Watching it, I think: *Grandma, Uncle Herbie, and Harris are all dead now.*

## 37

## Eleven Months, Two Weeks, Five Days

In Judaism, an unveiling is the ceremony that happens within a year of a loved one's death to formally dedicate the headstone. Prior to today, your grave was marked with a sad little sign that stuck out of the ground with your name typed in Arial font. Today we will go the cemetery for the unveiling. It's a beautiful day: clear blue skies, sixty-one degrees.

I was living in Manhattan when the Twin Towers fell: that was a beautiful day.

I got the call that you died last February: that was a beautiful day.

We go to the cemetery to unveil your headstone: another beautiful day.

Beautiful days scare the shit out of me now.

We plan to meet at the cemetery at 1:00 p.m. I haven't showered for a couple of days and decide it would be an appropriate time, but I'm dragging my feet. It usually takes me twenty minutes to get showered, dressed, and out the door. Today, it takes close to an hour. I stand in the shower so long the hot water turns cold.

After brushing my wet hair, I sit down for a while on the foot of the bed in my towel, blank. I get up, stare at all the clothes in my closet, and sit down a while longer. I'm having trouble breathing like I did sitting in the waiting room right before your funeral.

I start to sweat. My heart beats fast. I feel nauseous. I focus on my breathing to make sure it functions properly. I finally manage to put on a dress and two shoes and make my way downstairs and into the car. The drive over is relatively quiet. Iris eats peanut butter pretzels loudly in the back seat and eventually falls asleep a few minutes before we reach our destination.

When we pull into the cemetery, I see Mom and Dad, Taal, Matt Marcus, and Matt's girlfriend, Eby. Matt and Eby are wearing their purple "Harris" Phish T-shirts that they designed for the last Phish tour, the one you missed because you were here. They sold a ton of them.

We open our car doors gingerly so as not to wake the baby and head toward the covered headstone that sits underneath a shady tree. We quietly stand in a semi-circle around it, and Mom passes out copies of the short service she's created for her son who's buried beneath her feet. Meanwhile, Eby sits in the backseat of the car with Iris while she naps, her little mouth agape, completely safe from the sad scene on the other side of the car door, not fifty feet away.

Mom instructs us to read everything together. A few lines in, I blurt out, "*Aah!* I hate choral reading." I really do hate it. At various points, I drop out to cry. Mom does the same. Mike cries, too, but continues to read through the service. Dad reads quietly, inaudibly:

*We thank God for the gift of Harris who enriched our lives while he walked beside us.*

*We remember his memory in death even as we loved him in life.*

*We are grateful for the opportunity afforded us by this unveiling service to reach back into time and to remember the moments, days, and years we shared with Harris this day.*

*May his life indeed be bound up in the bond of everlasting life.*

*The greatest tribute is to remember his life:*

*In the rising of the sun and in its going down…We will remember him.*

*In the blowing of the wind and in the chill of winter… We will remember him.*

*In the opening of the buds and the rebirth of spring…We will remember him.*

*In the blueness of the sky and in the warmth of summer… We will remember.*

*In the rustling of leaves and in the beauty of autumn… We will remember him.*

*In the beginning of the year and when it ends…We will remember him.*

*When we are weary and in need of strength…We will remember him.*

*When we have joys we yearn to share…We will remember him.*

*When we gaze into Iris's eyes…We will remember him.*

*So long as we live, so he too shall live,*
*For he is part of us, part of our memory, part of our love.*


*The Lord is my shepherd, I shall not want.*
*God makes me lie down in green pastures.*
*God leads me beside the still waters to revive my spirit.*
*God guides me on the right path, for that is God's nature.*
*Though I walk in the valley of the shadow of death, I fear*
*no harm, for You are with me.*
*Your rod and your staff comfort me.*
*You prepare a banquet for me in the presence of my*
*enemies.*
*You anoint my head with oil; my cup overflows.*
*Surely goodness and kindness shall be my portion all the*
*days of my life.*
*And I shall dwell in the House of the Lord forever.*


As I read this passage aloud, I finally understand the meaning of the line about the valley of the shadow of death. Death is always present, always lurking. Death walks beside the living. I think about Samuel L. Jackson's monologue in *Pulp Fiction* and how he finally understood it, too, and in the midst of my trying to recall exactly what he said about it being some badass shit he used to say before he killed a motherfucker, it's time to uncover the headstone.

We kneel down and remove the heavy rocks weighing down the corners of the thin fabric that reads *Property of Congregation Emanu El.* There it is. A thick piece of engraved granite that will sit in this spot forever. We all take a moment to absorb it. A color photo of you is in the bottom left corner, the photo of you wearing the blue Maui cap that was taken at UCB, where you're looking so happy. On the opposite corner is the word "Harris" in the shape of the Phish logo, designed by your dear friend Rob Schrab. It's the same logo Matt and Eby wear on their shirts today:

There is a menorah positioned top center, sandwiched in between two Hebrew letters that mean *Here lies*. Hebrew on the headstone was important to Dad. The text beneath it reads:

*HARRIS LEE WITTELS*
*APRIL 20, 1984—FEBRUARY 19, 2015*
*THANKS FOR THE LAUGHS*

After removing the veil, we say the Mourner's Kaddish together. As much as I hate the awkwardness of choral reading, there is something so soothing about the ritual of a group of people saying Kaddish together.

*Yitgadal v'yitkadash sh'mei raba.*
*B'alma di v'ra chirutei*

*v'yamlich malchutei,*
*b'chayeichon uv'yomeichon*
*uv'chayei d'chol beit Yisrael,*
*baagala uviz'man kariv. V'im'ru: Amen.*
*Y'hei sh'mei raba m'varach*
*l'alam ul'almei almaya.*
*Yitbarach v'yishtabach v'yitpaar*
*v'yitromam v'yitnasei,*
*v'yit'hadar v'yitaleh v'yit'halal*
*sh'mei d'kud'sha b'rich hu,*
*l'eila min kol birchata v'shirata,*
*tushb'chata v'nechemata,*
*daamiran b'alma. V'imru: Amen.*
*Y'hei sh'lama raba min sh'maya,*
*v'chayim aleinu v'al kol Yisrael.*
*V'imru: Amen.*
*Oseh shalom bimromav,*
*Hu yaaseh shalom aleinu,*
*v'al kol Yisrael. V'imru: Amen.*

*Exalted and hallowed be God's great name in the world*
*which God created, according to plan.*
*May God's majesty be revealed in the days of our lifetime*
*and the life of all Israel—speedily, imminently, to which*
*we say: Amen.*
*Blessed be God's great name to all eternity.*
*Blessed, praised, honored, exalted, extolled, glorified,*
*adored, and lauded be the name of the Holy Blessed One,*
*beyond all earthly words and songs of blessing, praise,*

*and comfort. To which we say: Amen.*
*May there be abundant peace from heaven, and life, for*
*us and all Israel.*
*To which we say: Amen.*
*May the One who creates harmony on high, bring peace*
*to us and to all Israel.*
*To which we say: Amen.*

When it's over, we line the headstone with stones we've brought. In Judaism, it's customary to bring stones in lieu of flowers. Flowers eventually die; a stone does not. Earlier today, Iris decorated the stone I brought in this gold paint pen that wasn't washable and is now essentially hennaed all over her body. The stone is smooth and gray. It's the one she took from outside your house in Los Feliz when we went last year to clean it out. So now a piece of Los Feliz is resting on top of you.

Mom lays down an evil eye and a rock with an engraved frog on it. She collects frogs. She has hundreds of them. Neither of us ever understood why. (Please note: I still don't.)

Taal bends down and kisses your headstone with his lips. Very Taal.

Dad walks away and sits on a bench, alone. Very Dad.

I quote a couple of lines from the graveyard scene in *Steel Magnolias* in a thick Southern accent: "He will always be young, he will always be beautiful." Very me.

And then this odd thing happens: we just start having a totally normal conversation, standing over your grave. Matt throws out some ideas for the name of a new pizza restaurant he's opening. We all vote for Twittels Pizza after your Twitter handle, @twittels, a clever mash-up of Twitter and Wittels. You really were top-notch at the internet.

Mom tells us there's a whole new body of research that AA doesn't work and medical intervention is the way to go with heroin addiction. I ask her why she keeps reading about this stuff. She says she can't stop. I ask if it makes her feel better. She says it makes her feel *much* worse.

"If he just could have held out for a couple more years," she says for the hundredth time.

"Mom, he was who he was. He was always gonna do what he was gonna do."

Taal tells us that the main character in Louis C.K.'s new internet series is named Horace Wittel. In the series, the character died a year ago. They apparently take great pains in the show to enunciate the word *Wittel* like we Wittels have to do.

We talk about *Friday Night Lights,* the box set of which the boys have brought and laid next to your headstone along with a Phish CD, a children's book called *God Gave Us You*, dozens of fresh flowers, and some tiny, plastic toy soldiers, red and blue and yellow.

We kiss our fingertips and touch them to the headstone.

We walk back to the car to lovingly stare at the sleeping baby.

Then we all drive to Kenny & Ziggy's Delicatessen, where we drown our sorrows in piles of corned beef and heaps of chopped liver.

# 38

—

## A Week Before

### February 2015

My brother and I had our last phone conversation eight days before he died. It was the last time I would ever hear his voice in real time. Had I known, I would have stayed on the phone with him forever. Or at least for much longer than I did. The conversation was so brief and insignificant.

He called to hash out an angsty Facebook status I'd just posted about the unsolicited feedback I often get in public about Iris's hearing aids.

Some answers to some common questions posed by strangers upon noticing Iris's hearing aids:

"What's wrong with her ears?" Nothing is wrong with her ears. Her ears are perfect—unlike you. You are a rude asshole.

"Can she hear?" Yes, you fool. She's wearing hearing aids. That is the point. Do you think this is a fashion statement I am making?

"Does she have to wear those forever?" Yep. Every single waking hour of every single day for the rest of her life. There is no cure for hearing loss. It is a permanent condition. *And* it has taken me lots of time, tears, and hard work to finally come to a place of acceptance about all that. But thanks for kicking that dust up for me. It's really something I wanted to dig into—again—with you.

A few minutes later, the phone rang and *Harris Wittels* showed up on the caller ID. No matter what I was doing, I always picked up the phone when I saw his name.

"Man, you went *HAM* on Facebook," he said when I answered.

"What is a *ham*?"

"Hard as a motherfucker?" He said it judgmentally, like I should know this.

"Well, people are fucking idiots."

"Yeah, but they mean well. They're just trying to connect with you and understand it—they just don't know what to say. No one ever knows what to say about anything."

And just like that, I was disarmed. He really was the only one who could tell me to calm the fuck down in a way that felt loving and nonthreatening. He was the one who could talk me off a ledge because he'd seen me stand on so many ledges so many times before. Siblings know you from the beginning. They know how you react to pain, setbacks, disappointment, hurt, and sadness. They know how to say the thing that will cut right through all the bullshit and diffuse the situation. Or, conversely, the thing that will exacerbate the situation, if that's the goal. Like the thing Harris always used to do in the car where he would put his finger a millimeter away from my arm and say, "I'm not touching you, I'm not touching you," and I would want to rip the finger right off of his hand.

*Who will be able to fill that space now?*

On February 13, Harris texted: More vids please [of Iris]. I've watched the new ones a thousand times. I sensed a sort of desperation. It was as if he was saying, *I need this. I need a reason. I need a thing to make me keep going or I'm not going to make it.*

Why didn't I say something?

The last video I sent him was the one of Iris walking for the first time. It was two days before he died. When I recovered his phone from the coroner's office, I saw a picture of Iris on his lock screen.

## 39

## Eleven Months, Three Weeks, Six Days

A few days before the anniversary of your death, I wake up with the real-ization that I need to buy a yahrzeit candle. In Judaism, it's the memo-rial candle that's lit every year on the anniversary of a loved one's death. I search Amazon and read reviews. I can't fathom having the time or energy to write a review on *anything*, but reviewing a yahrzeit candle feels especially odd. Nevertheless, I read them. People seem to favor one that comes in a blue tin because it's cheaper. Jews. I think about that one joke you always used to tell about Jews. You'd come out onstage and confidently exclaim in this sort of sing-songy voice, "Jews love money!" Then you'd hold for a beat and say, "I can say that because…I hate Jews."

I buy a six-pack (of candles) as well as an electric one that you plug into an outlet. I don't know why I would need both, but I want to be prepared.

I feel nauseous again. I breathe deeply to calm the sick inside my body. I'm having what feels like an extended, slow-motion panic attack over several days. Is this a thing? I try to pack my lunch but feel queasy looking in the fridge at all the food. I sit on the couch and put my feet up. I close my eyes. Iris is dancing around the room in her polka-dot rain boots, holding her mermaid doll. Mike is in the background asking if I want an ice pack. I respond to neither.

I look up at the bookshelves. On the top shelf is this 11-inch by 17-inch poster that's mounted on foam board. It's a blown-up *Apples to Apples* playing card that reads *Harris Wittels: 1984–American actor, comedian, writer, and musician. Known for authoring* Humblebrag: The Art of False Modesty; *Also possesses a deep, unwavering affection for Phish.* No death date was listed. You used to love playing *Apples to Apples.* I wonder when this was made and why. I wonder so much about the origins of all your shit. Two shelves over is the framed photo of you in your Maui baseball cap that's now also on your headstone. Also on the top shelf is an 8-inch by 10-inch painting on canvas by a fan of your character Harris, the animal control guy, from *Parks and Rec*. Four shelves down is a black-and-white Wittels family photo that we took at Ganny's eighty-ninth birthday party, where you're awkwardly touching my shoulder and Mom and I are mid-cackle. Next to that is a small photo of us standing back-to-back, arms crossed like Milli Vanilli or some other group in a late 1980s music video. I'm seventeen; you're fourteen. We took it in our backyard for Mother's Day one year. My hair is dyed fire-engine red because I was in *The Miss Firecracker Contest* at the time. This little, gold-framed photo of us sat on the bookshelf in the living room at your house in LA, and now it sits here with the rest of your displaced shit.

I sit on the couch and absorb all of the you that's in front of me. It's pushing a lot of buttons. I finally take a good, deep breath, and the tears pour out. I try to muffle them, so Iris doesn't get upset, but I can't. Mike comes behind me and hugs my neck. Iris comes over and lays her head on my legs, looks in my eyes and grins. She gives me a pat-pat-pat.

I say, "Remember what I told you about when your friends are sad? What do you say when your friend is sad?"

She says, "You need hug?"

I say, "Yes, baby, I need hug." And she does.

I keep saying it, but it's true again and again: it's hard to wallow in misery when this creature is staring back at me. This is why I kept sending you videos and photos of her and why you kept asking for videos and photos of her. She is the best medicine. I feel less nauseous after staring into my daughter's eyes and finally breathing into the place that hurts, and I'm able to move on with my day. I do have one more hysterical, explosive, crying fit once I get to work, which hasn't happened in a while, but it is what it is. I'm dreading the end of this week. We all are.

Later that evening, Iris's speech therapist sends us an email with the results of the speech evaluation we did earlier that week. It was the first time Iris actually performed the test herself. On previous occasions, Mike and I would answer a bunch of questions and the therapist would use them to score her progress. According to the report, Iris scored higher than 90 percent of kids her age. At two years old, she is "performing similarly to a three-year-old," which means she's on a three-year-old level of a child with typical hearing.

I think back to all those initial questions that plagued me when she was first born:

Will her voice be affected? *No.*

Can she hear birds chirping with hearing aids? Whispering? *Yes.*

Concerts, music classes, dance classes, movie theaters, airplanes? *She does it all.*

Can she hear us if we call for her from the other room? *Yes.*

Do we have to be looking at her when we talk? *No. She has supersonic hearing.*

Daycare with hearing kids or special school? *She's in daycare with all hearing kids.*
Mainstream education? *Yep, headed that direction.*
What can she hear now? *Everything. She can hear everything. Calm the fuck down.*

I think about how devastated I was when you came home a few weeks after she was born, how you said it was the most depressed you'd ever seen me. I think about how worried I was about her future—that she would fall behind, that she would suffer, that all of it would be so hard. I think about how you told me to stop "future-tripping," that Iris would be just fine—better than fine. She was just a chill baby. I was the one who was fucked-up about it. Not her. I want to go back in time and talk to myself and tell that terrified new mom that everything is going to be okay. I want to tell her, "Your child is a wonder. That's all you need to know."

I celebrate my child's success, and I yearn to share it with you.

I often wonder when all of this will end, but there is no end to grief. There's only navigating the way to a new normal. The old normal consisted of us being a family of four, then a family of five, then a family of six. In the old normal, we texted each other constantly about Iris, about girls, about television shows. We told each other secrets and compared notes on Mom and Dad. In the old normal, we constantly worried about whether you were sober, using, alive or dead, and you constantly reassured us that you had it under control.

On February 19, 2015, you died of a drug overdose. You were thirty years old. You were talented. You were successful. You were loved.

Time is now measured before and after that day.

I remember thinking at the time that I would never feel joy again. I was wrong. I often smile without guilt or hesitation. I play hide and seek. I make small talk, paint portraits, sing songs, buy groceries and cook things with them. I co-parent a flock of baby dolls and pick fresh strawberries with my toddler. I've shared a bottle of wine with friends. I directed a couple of plays. I survived being stranded outside of a gas station 'til 4:00 a.m. after a flash flood. I worked to get a bill passed in the Texas Legislature that didn't pass because Texas is the worst, but the point is, I tried.

Sometimes we even eat pizza and dance in the living room to reggae music and Annie Lennox. I never expected to dance in the living room again. I still post too many pictures of Iris on the internet, but my God, she is just the funniest little person. She makes me laugh a hundred times a day, a thousand times a week, a million times a month. And what better way to honor you than to laugh? So, I'm going to continue doing that. And as time passes—as it inevitably does—the good days will outnumber the bad.

Now I find you in places I never looked before. Like today, I saw multiple clouds in the sky shaped like fish and knew it was you. Or yesterday, when a white feather blew across the floor of my office, and I picked it up gingerly and laid it on the bookshelf over my desk. Or a month ago, when this gnarly possum crossed our fence in the backyard three days in a row at 5:45 p.m. like he was coming home from a long day at the office and Mom proclaimed it was "the spirit of Harris."

Your absence will always be palpable but so will your spirit, your presence, your memory.

This is the new normal.

# 40
—

## One Year

*He's dead.*
*He died.*
*Your brother died.*
*He is dead.*


A year has passed.
It feels like yesterday and a hundred years ago all at the same time.


I leave work early to beat rush-hour traffic, and Mike drives us to the cemetery. We bring flowers. We tidy up the area. I brush off all the ants that are crawling on the headstone and all over the *Friday Night Lights* box set. I prop up all the little toy soldiers. I fall to my knees. I show you a few videos of Iris. I tell you how much I miss you. I tell you how much I hate you. I tell you how much I love you. It's hard to walk away. It's hard to know what to say. Every time I come here, I don't know what to say. Every time I come here, I have trouble walking away.

After the cemetery, we pick up Iris from preschool, and I breathe her in like she's an oxygen mask on a plummeting airplane. The babysitter arrives at 5:30 p.m., and Mike and I head back out to meet Dad at the synagogue. Mom won't be joining us for the service because she opted for a weekend trip to New Orleans with her best friend, Kay. I don't blame her. Everyone has to grieve in her own way. I wouldn't want to be here for my kid's Yahrzeit either.

Even though we're here for the shittiest of reasons, the service is notably upbeat, featuring a mini jam-band. There are bongos and a tambourine. You'd like it. I lean over to Mike at some point and tell him we should bring Iris. Like you, she goes bonkers over live music.

At the end of the service, the rabbi reads a list of congregants who died this week. I think about how ripped apart I was last year when we sat in this service. I think about the families who are sitting here today, how ripped apart they must be. Then he reads the list of congregants who died this week in years past. The list is exceptionally long and alphabetical, so we have lots of time until we get to the W's. When your name finally comes out of his mouth, I spill tears, lots of tears. It's hard to catch my breath. I cry through the Kaddish. I'm unable to say it. I look up at the ceiling and wonder if you're looking down.

I think about the day a person dies, how the morning is just a morning, a meal is just a meal, a song is just a song. It's not the *last* morning, or the *last* meal, or the *last* song. It's all very ordinary, and then it's all very over.

The space between life and death is a moment.

Last February 19 was an ordinary day. I took some photos of my baby flipping through a thick book called *Lost Beauties of the English Language.* I made coffee, drove to work, taught my students, ate some lunch. I noted the beautiful day. I met my family at speech therapy. After my daughter's session, I changed her diaper like I'd done a thousand times before.

All the while, you lay lifeless on a rug a thousand miles away, and I had no idea. Until I got the call, I had no idea. In one moment you were alive, and in the next, you weren't. That fast. In one moment I was myself, and in the next, I wasn't.

Because a huge part of my identity is being your sister.

And while it was over for you in a moment (at least I hope it was that fast), it will remain alive in me for hundreds of thousands of future moments. I am forever changed by something that happened to you in a moment.

The Greeks called it a *peripeteia*: a sudden reversal of fortune or change in circumstances. A point of no return.

I wonder what led up to your point of no return.

I wonder about the first thing you thought when you opened your eyes that morning.

I wonder what you ate for breakfast, for lunch, for dinner. I hope one of them was Chili's nachos. Or a plate of melted string cheese. Or the chocolatey bottom of a Drumstick.

I wonder what Phish or Alkaline Trio or Islands songs you heard while driving in your black car with the windows down, smoking a cigarette, wearing your Ray-Bans.

I wonder what jokes were brewing inside your head.

I wonder if you watched any adorable videos of your niece and, if so, which ones.

I wonder what plans you made for later that day and for tomorrow.

I wonder what you thought about before you did the thing that changed all of us forever.

I wonder if, despite the bruise on the inside of your arm, you were happy.

The 5:45 p.m. possum that Mom deemed your spirit animal stopped coming around a few weeks ago. But this morning at 9:30 a.m., as I sipped my morning coffee while staring out the window, I saw three possums strut back and forth across the back fence, one of them carrying a baby on its back.

So, it turns out that Mom was right. Your spirit *is* alive and well and living in the shape of a possum.

# 41
—

## One Year, One Day

I carry the most painful memories inside my muscles and bones. I remember falling to the ground on the bathroom floor. Pounding my fists on the pavement. Sitting on my knees in the dirt next to a hole in the ground. Standing exposed on a pulpit before hundreds of people, reading these horrible words aloud:

> *I want to say that we will never get over this loss, that it has ruined our family, torn us apart, and left us all bloody and begging for mercy—that our hearts have left our bodies and will be buried in the ground today. That there will always be a gaping, painful hole in our family and a feeling that something isn't right, that no holiday, vacation, meal, or conversation will ever be the same.*
>
> *I want to say that I don't know how I will continue to exist in the world in the same way ever again. But, I know if Harris were listening—and I have to pray that he is out there listening, continuing to be our tour guide through the cosmos—that he would tell me to stop future-tripping, to just be in this moment today.*
>
> *So, I will say that today, I miss my brother more than I can*

*possibly explain. Today, I am devastated and sad and angry and empty. Today, I long to bring him back and fix things and try to understand. Today, I would pay a million dollars to hear him laugh or say hi, sister, to see that one self-conscious smile that he always wore. Today, I love my brother with all of my being. And I always will.*

Today.

Today is my birthday.

Today is my birthday that will forever fall the day after you died.

I lie in bed for several moments in the quiet before putting my feet on the floor. Mike has let me sleep in. The dog is curled up in his nook beside me. I reach for my phone by the bedside table. The Facebook Happy Birthday messages are in full swing. Mom says: "Hope it's a decent 35th birthday my special, kind, sensitive, beautiful daughter. I adore you and am beyond proud of all that you have become. You are so strong in your convictions and such an amazing mom. You were the best sister on earth. He was so lucky to have you. Let's hold hands and keep moving forward. Our loving family bond will help. It has to. I love you."

Last year, Facebook confused the condolence messages with the birthday messages, so every time I logged on, I was greeted with an exploding graphic of balloons and confetti. I lie there and think: *Why didn't I turn these comments off?*

After a few minutes of staring at the ceiling fan, I head downstairs. There are flowers on the dining room table and a colorful drawing by the tiny artist who lives in my house. The note in Magic Marker says: "To the best mommy in the world on her birthday. Love, Iris 2016." She's watching *The Princess Bride,* your favorite childhood movie. Well, maybe second to *Pee-wee's Big Adventure*. As a kid, you compulsively did the dance Pee-wee does in the biker bar scene to the song "Tequila." I can still hear Mom squealing, "Harris, do the dance! Do the dance!" It always brought the house down. Third place for favorite childhood movie was definitely *Labyrinth*. When you were Iris's age, you would watch these movies on repeat. They would end and you would demand that Mom rewind the tapes and play them again and again and again. Iris does this, too, now.

I'm immediately greeted with a smothering hug and "Mommy! Mommy! Mommy! Mommy! Mommy! Mommy! Mommy!" I sit on the couch. Mike wraps his arms around me. We watch the scene in the fire swamp with the ROUS's (Rodents of Unusual Size). Bursts of fire erupt every few steps that Westley and Buttercup take. Iris tells us "That's fire! Make pizza!" Pizza ovens are her only frame of reference for a flame that large.

I'm sandwiched between my husband to my left and my daughter to my right and we're watching TV in our pajamas and tears form in my eyes when I think of you, and I take a deep breath and look out the window and see the blue sky and the clouds moving along and a bird flying, and then three more, and I think: *Life is happening all around me.*

I have Iris. And Mike. And Mom. And Dad. And Wiley, the dog. And my friends. And my students. And the sun. And the sky.

Life is happening all around me.

When we were little, Benihana was your favorite birthday destination. You liked wearing the tall red hat and haggling the chef. The last time we came here together on Christmas Eve, 2013, you took a photo of our chef and posted it on Instagram with a caption that read: "Houston Benihana. They made this Mexican guy be called Chan. I ain't buyin it." While I don't want to celebrate my birthday, I don't want Dad to be alone for dinner. Mom is away on her "I'm Gonna Do Whatever I Want Because My Son Died and I Fucking Deserve It" Girl's Trip, and we all have to eat. So, Benihana it is.

At dinner, Dad and I go through two bottles of sake. Iris is riveted by the cooking show or attempting to shovel rice into her mouth with chopsticks or curled up on the ground with her rain boots kicked off her feet watching this weird Canadian clown show called *The Big Comfy Couch* on my iPhone. Mike has gotten me a white cake with white icing and colorful sprinkles that simply says: *Day*. The waitress brings it over in a giant, pink box. She lights a single candle. The birthday song is sung. I make a wish and blow out my candle. Iris "helps" and keeps saying "Mommy Happy Birthday!" She loves birthdays. It's not so bad.

Last year on my birthday, I invited friends to a tiki bar down the street, but we never made it. Tonight, some of those friends casually inform me that they're going to the tiki bar later, and I can go, or not go, they don't care. Either way, they'll be there. After dinner, Dad offers to stay with the baby, and we decide to go even though I feel guilty about it. I didn't intend to celebrate. But then we get in the car and it's all '90s music on the radio, and I sing along with volume and commitment in spite of myself.

Once we're there, scrunched into a booth in the back of the bar drinking colorful drinks out of shells that are lit on fire, all the negative noise fades away. I hold Mike's hand and make filthy jokes and take photos of my friends and post them on Instagram. Surrounded by great people and Hawaiian decor, I feel like myself again. I feel like the person who inhabited my body before The Tragedy.

After leaving the bar, we head to my friend's for a nightcap. I sprawl out on a lounge chair on the deck and eat greasy potato chips out of a giant bag to the searing sounds of midnight burgers on the grill. We drink beers and listen to music and talk about moisturizer. I show my friends a YouTube video of a relatively thin woman completing the 72-ounce steak challenge twice in twenty minutes at this restaurant in Amarillo, Texas. She literally ate ten pounds of food and broke a world record.

As Mike and I walk back to the car, I think, *I'm tired of feeling shitty. I don't want to feel this way anymore.*

When I get home, drunk, I say this out loud to Dad: "Dad, I want to live again."

"That's progress," he says.

Yesterday, we lit a Yahrzeit candle that sat on the kitchen counter and burned brightly in memory of you. We will light a Yahrzeit candle every year on this day. And every year, it will burn out on my birthday. And every year, that cruel juxtaposition will remind me that life is moving on without you.

This is how it is now: equal parts joy and sorrow. Everything all at once.

I have this vivid memory of driving with Iris to the grocery store last summer on a particularly dark day. It's one of those seemingly insignificant moments that made a permanent mark. "You Are My Sunshine" shuffled onto Pandora Toddler Radio. Glancing at Iris in the rearview mirror, I was simultaneously overwhelmed with pure joy as I saw her singing and clapping along and sorrow that you would never get to see such a spectacular view.

*You are my sunshine, my only sunshine.*
*You make me happy when skies are gray.*
*You'll never know, dear, how much I love you.*
*Please don't take my sunshine away.*

*The other night dear when I lay sleeping,*
*I dreamed I held you in my arms.*
*When I awoke dear, I was mistaken,*
*So I hung my head and cried.*

This song is so happy and sad at once. It's what it feels like to be alive. It's what it feels like to lose someone you love but still be surrounded by so much light.

# 42

—

## Epilogue

Change and movement is inevitable. Unstoppable. And tragedy can function like fuel.

After surviving The Tragedy, I realized I didn't give a shit about outcomes in the same way I used to give a shit about outcomes. Because when someone you love with all your being suddenly drops dead, it's a reminder of a few things:

1. We aren't in control.
2. Time is running out.
3. Nothing matters.

At first, the nothing matters was a sinking ship or a mound of quicksand or a pile of rubble where I sat, paralyzed, for months and months. There wasn't much to do during that time except for the Irish keening and the crying and the occasional pounding of my fists on the floor. You read the book. But after 365 days of *grief*, my tears dried up long enough to lift my head and survey the damage, and I realized, *I don't have to sit here forever.*

It's uncomfortable—even painful—to live on a pile of rubble. Not sustainable. Unsafe. Devoid of plumbing and pillows. And since nothing mattered anymore (see above), the stakes felt lower in a way. Like I could do anything I wanted to do and be anything I wanted to be. I could revise the script. I *had to*. Because I was no longer myself.

My debilitating sadness started morphing into something empowering. Positive. A freedom and a courage that I'd never really felt to make the most of the time I *do* have.

I started to look at all the things that were weighing me down even before Harris died, the stuff I'd shoved into overstuffed drawers and hidden in the part of my brain, heart, and gut that I was too tired and scared to acknowledge. And I slowly started to piece together a new identity, one that didn't include Harris but was happening as a direct result of his absence. His untimely death was inspiring me to live.

As a kid, when I looked into my future, I saw a successful theater artist doing successful theater artist things. I was so certain of my career path at seventeen that I only applied to NYU because the internet said it was the best. And they took me! And even though I did well there and people seemed to believe in me, I gave up before I even tried. I got scared by 9/11 and didn't want to take headshots because I *felt* ten pounds overweight and couldn't figure out how to balance the drain of a day job with something more creative and meaningful. I had no energy for anything creative and meaningful because I was doing a daily commute of over an hour each way from Queens to the Upper West Side to wipe actual butts at a preschool for rich babies.

Nothing was working, so I abandoned my plan.

I left New York, moved back to Texas, and made smart and practical choices. I got a stable job teaching *other* people how to be creative, which looked great on paper, but after ten years was no longer fulfilling in a way that was enough. The loss of my passion and creativity was palpable and draining, and unfortunately, something I rediscovered once I started writing out of desperation for four, sometimes five, hours a night about the death of my brother. It's fucked-up but true.

Once I started writing and processing and dissecting my mountain of sadness, I realized it made no sense to be smart and practical if I was miserable. I knew now that I could die at any point, in an instant. Everyone *knows* that, but you don't *really* know that until you see it up close in your own backyard. And it made me want to tear the walls down and build something new, to do something with my time that made me feel inspired and inspired others.

So, I quit my job. And it felt good. For the first time in my life, I didn't second-guess my decision.

Around the same time, I partnered up with a friend who I'd sat down with ten years earlier to daydream about opening an arts space in Houston. It made little sense at the time since we were both basically children with no money. But right around the time I quit my job, he found the perfect space, and we decided to take the risk, to turn this dream into a reality. It's important to note that it still made little sense since both of us are theater people with no prior experience either opening or running a business, but we did it anyway because nothing matters, remember? I understood it could be a disaster but truly didn't give a shit. What's the worst thing that happens? It fails? So what. That's not the worst thing that could happen. I survived the worst thing that could happen. I can survive anything. I'm a fucking champion.

So, I invested a portion of the money Harris left me in a space for comedians, musicians, dancers, actors, directors, podcasters, renegades, and artists of every kind to incubate, create, and work. In June 2016, we opened the doors to Rec Room, a multidisciplinary performance space and bar in downtown Houston. Six months later, we launched a nonprofit arts organization called Rec Room Arts that continues to support and provide space for both established and up-and-coming artists.

The name is an intentional nod to *Parks and Rec*; the space, an homage to Harris. Without him, it wouldn't exist. At the risk of crossing the line into hypersentimentality, Harris was my hero. Fear wasn't part of his genetic makeup. He was a bona fide risk-taker who always followed his dreams. What better way to honor him than to follow my own?

On Harris's birthday, April 20, we partnered with 8th Wonder Brewery, owned and operated by Harris's three childhood best friends, to launch the 1st Annual Harris Phest. Hundreds of people showed up. A Phish cover band played. Stand-up comedians performed. We ate a white sheet cake with white icing from the grocery store.

Today, a framed needlepoint portrait of Harris with the caption *We're All Horrible and Wonderful and Figuring It Out* hangs on the wall of the bar.

He's always with me there.

Some other cool notable things happened too:

After six exhausting months and *literally* fifty steps in the Texas Legislature, including committee hearings and nearly unanimous votes in both the House and Senate, the governor of Texas finally signed H.B. 490 into law on June 15, 2017. Effective September 1, 2017, hearing aids and cochlear implants for children under eighteen will be covered by insurance. In total, it took six years and three legislative sessions to make this happen. Like I said, fuel. Lots of fuel.

I started a weekly parenting podcast called *Hands Off Parents*.

I edited and edited and edited and finally finished this book.

I put on eyeliner.

I ate a salad.

I went on vacation with my two favorite people, Mike and Iris, and we drove through the mountains with the windows rolled down, enveloped by the pine-scented air. I thought of my brother. I held him in my cells. I felt the vulnerability of the altitude and the winding road and the walls of rocks towering above us. I noted how small I was compared to the sky. I saw that the world is beautiful. I heard my daughter say, "Wow." And I felt grateful.

Granted, I still have bad days. Sometimes I have *really* bad days. I often stand at the kitchen counter and shovel cold spaghetti down my throat. Because I still miss my brother. That never fades. And there are days when I'm teleported right back into the rubble, and it takes me hours, days, sometimes weeks, to climb back out. Also, as if I were a video game, opening a new business with no prior experience has unlocked a whole new level of stress and anxiety that feels impossible to beat. Quitting my job felt great initially, but businesses take time to grow, and now we worry about money, health insurance, and retirement constantly. I also worry about climate change and gun control and women's rights and police brutality and political doom and nuclear war. I still worry about Iris's hearing loss, albeit far more infrequently than I used to, but it's still a frequency in my mind. And as the saying goes, raising an empowered woman means you have to deal with an empowered woman. My sweet child is now an empowered "threenager" who refuses to listen most of the time and tantrums her way through 50 percent of her life. And I miss the mark on responding to her in a positive way 50 percent of the time. Parenting is hard.

But I'm doing the best that I can. We're all doing the best we can. And while I can't say the ending is a happy one that fits nicely in a gift-wrapped box, I *can* say that I've gotten to the point where the good days outweigh the bad, and that's something. I didn't stay in the rubble. I climbed out, and I moved forward.

A huge part of what helped me move forward was writing this book. When the pain was too much to bear, I wrote it down, and it kept me going. When I was writing it, I wasn't thinking about what I was writing or whether it would be published or who would read it or how it would be received. I just wrote from the bottom of my guts about everything that was going on in this nightmare of a moment. I wrote the truth. And, often, the truth is ugly. This is why Instagram has filters.

My biggest fear in putting all of this out there is that I am dishonoring my brother and making him look bad by telling this part of his story. This is the last thing I'd ever want to do. It keeps me up at night. But people are flawed, and addiction is ugly, unflattering, and unapologetic. It's a disease that has stolen hundreds of thousands of innocent lives, and the numbers are climbing. This is a story that starts with addiction and ends with grief. There's no way to sugarcoat that. It's what happened. And, ultimately, it's the story I had to tell.

However, I hope it's also clear from the book that Harris was the most incredible person I've ever known. And everyone who knew him felt this way. Like I said in my eulogy, he made the rest of us look bad. He was the funniest. He was the coolest. He had the most creative, inventive, limitless mind that was perpetually working. He was a true and tremendous talent who accomplished more in thirty years than most people accomplish in a lifetime. This is the Harris everyone will remember. And this is why this story is so unbearably tragic.

Mike and I are trying to have another baby. There's nothing more hopeful than that, right? New life. When it happens, if it happens, we will name the baby after the boy who hung the moon: Harris.

# Acknowledgments

Thank you first and foremost to my supportive, thoughtful, selfless, wonderful, strange husband who loves me through it *all*—the horrible, the wonderful, and every (rarely) dull moment in between. I wouldn't be me without Mike. He's the one who sat me down one day and introduced me to a website called Medium where I could pour out all of my feelings. He actively encouraged me to start writing and has stuck with me through every idea, draft, and painstaking revision from that point forward. I love you, Mike.

Thanks to Kate Lee at Medium for connecting me with my agent Rachel Sussman, without whom *none* of this would be happening. Rachel found an essay I'd posted, reached out to see if I had any desire to turn it into a memoir, and now many, many, *many* revisions later, here we are. I owe her a mountain of gratitude for guiding me through every step of this process. I am so fortunate to now have a stellar literary agent and an even better friend.

Thanks to my editor Shana Drehs for her patience, collaboration, and endless support along the way. This book wouldn't be what it is without her talent and insight. I am so grateful to Shana and everyone at Sourcebooks for seeing the potential in this story and taking a chance on me! Thanks also to Liz Kelsch for all of her help on the PR front!

Thank you to my dear friends Chloe Gonzalez, Abby Koenig, and Jennifer Mathieu for reading drafts along the way and, more importantly, for always being in my corner.

Thank you to Aziz Ansari, Sarah Silverman, Mike Schur, Louis C.K., Jeff Ullrich, and Sarah Rayne for allowing me to publish your words, but more importantly for the love you showed my brother. Thanks to Rob Schrab and Robyn Von Swank for the powerful images. Thanks to Kulap & Scott, Dave Becky, Susan Hale, Michael & Deanna, Paul & Lesley, Tig Notaro, Alan Yang, Matt Marcus, Taal Douadi, Armen Weitzman, Danny Molad, Annie Stein, and the one and only Johnny Smith for always being there for the Wittels family.

Thanks to everyone in LA who showed up with boxes, packing tape, and love to help us pack up Harris's house. It's a kindness we will never forget.

Thanks to NBC for the assistance along the way.

Thank you to my wonderful in-laws, extended family, HSPVA family, and Rec Room family for all your love and support.

Thanks to Ganny and Grandma, who are no longer here in body but always here in spirit.

Iris once told me we have a bucket in our hearts, and that the people you love and who love you fill up your bucket. If that's true, thanks to my amazing mom and dad for filling my bucket to the brim with a lifetime of unconditional love, support, laughter, and the courage to do what inspires me. Harris always used to say that we had great parents and that our childhood was perfect. It's totally true. From the moment we opened our eyes, our parents pushed us to be authentically ourselves and to chase all of our crazy dreams. They paved the way, and I love them tremendously.

A special thanks to my dad for bleeding red ink on every paper I ever wrote growing up. In response to the question you posed after you read something I'd written years ago, "Yes, Dad, I do have to put an adjective before every noun."

Thank you to my hilarious, sweet, and mighty little girl, Iris. I don't understand how all of that personality fits into such a tiny body, but somehow it does. You are so special, and I am so proud of you. Thank you for saving my life and giving me a reason again and again and again every single day. You are my hero, baby girl, and I love you so.

And, finally, thank you, Harris, for being my brother. I won the sibling lottery when you were born. You are my favorite. Always have been. Always will be. Keep gettin' down on that ice cream buffet... until we meet again.

# About the Author

Stephanie Wittels Wachs is a writer whose work has been featured on Vox, Longform, Huffington Post, Fatherly, Mamamia, Babble, and Medium. Other significant roles include mother, theatre artist, educator, and voice actor. She graduated from New York University's Tisch School of the Arts and went on to receive her master's from the University of Houston School of Theatre and Dance.  She is cofounder of Rec Room Arts, a nonprofit arts organization committed to developing innovative work across disciplines. Find her comedic musings on parenting (and life) on her weekly podcast, *Hands Off Parents*. She lives in Houston, Texas, with her family.